Praise for
CRAFT DISTILLING

Craft Distilling accomplishes the extraordinary task of making the arcane art form accessible and practical for anyone who can cook from a recipe. The joy of creating spirits at home is a great incentive for learning a little chemistry and Victoria makes the chemistry fun!
—Bryan Welch, *Mother Earth News* , and CEO, B the Change Media

In *Craft Distilling*, author Victoria Redhed Miller leads us on a wonderfully intoxicating journey that answers the question of why distill spirits at home with eloquence and clarity that only a passionate practitioner can offer. With Miller's help we come to understand just why it is that most of us can't legally make spirits for ourselves, and she makes a wonderful case for why we should be able to do just that! Set the history aside for a spell and *Craft Distilling* delves deeply into the science of alcohol distillation and sets you up with everything from detailed recipes for your favorite liquors and insight on constructing your own still. *Craft Distilling* is as important for dreamers and practitioners as it is for policy makers, and it belongs on the shelf of everyone who has anything to do with the production and consumption of distilled spirits.
—Oscar H. Will III, Editorial Director, *Mother Earth News*

This is one of the most comprehensive books I have seen to date. This book tells you everything you need to know to become a knowledgeable distiller. The book also has many great recipe's. I would highly recommend this book to any new or experienced distiller.
—Mike Haney, Hillbilly Stills

CRAFT DISTILLING

MAKING LIQUOR LEGALLY *at* HOME

Victoria Redhed Miller

new society
PUBLISHERS

Cover design by Diane McIntosh.
Cover main image © iStock: Zakharova_Natalia
Printed in Canada. First printing January 2016.

Funded by the
Government
of Canada

Financé par le
gouvernement
du Canada

Canada

Inquiries regarding requests to reprint all or part of *Craft Distilling*
should be addressed to New Society Publishers at the address below.
To order directly from the publishers, please call toll-free (North America)
1-800-567-6772, or order online at www.newsociety.com

Any other inquiries can be directed by mail to:

New Society Publishers
P.O. Box 189, Gabriola Island, BC V0R 1X0, Canada
(250) 247-9737

LIBRARY AND ARCHIVES CANADA CATALOGUING IN PUBLICATION

Miller, Victoria Redhed, author
Craft distilling : making liquor legally at home / Victoria
Redhed Miller.

Includes bibliographical references and index.
Issued in print and electronic formats.
ISBN 978-0-86571-804-3 (paperback).—ISBN 978-1-55092-604-0 (ebook)

1. Liquors—Amateurs' manuals.   2. Distillation—Amateurs' manuals.
I. Title.

TP597.M54 2016   663'.16   C2015-906495-3
                                         C2015-906496-1

New Society Publishers' mission is to publish books that contribute in fundamental
ways to building an ecologically sustainable and just society, and to do so with the
least possible impact on the environment, in a manner that models this vision. We
are committed to doing this not just through education, but through action. The
interior pages of our bound books are printed on Forest Stewardship Council®-
registered acid-free paper that is 100% post-consumer recycled (100% old growth
forest-free), processed chlorine-free, and printed with vegetable-based, low-VOC
inks, with covers produced using FSC®-registered stock. New Society also works to
reduce its carbon footprint, and purchases carbon offsets based on an annual audit
to ensure a carbon neutral footprint. For further information, or to browse our full
list of books and purchase securely, visit our website at: **www.newsociety.com**

For David, my wonderful husband and partner in homesteading.
Thank you for being so supportive of all my projects,
for encouraging me to pursue my passions
and for always being available at a moment's notice
for emergency taste-testing.

Here's to all who refined their craft
and perfected their skills as home distillers;
may your spirit live on in those of us
aiming for a world of good spirits and sensible rules.

Contents

Sanity Finally Comes To Moonshine Phobia

by Gene Logsdon

Should you be so optimistic as to think you can figure out why human beings are mostly crazy, study the history of intoxicating beverages. I do not mean just the miseries that result from drunkenness which kills or maims more people and wrecks more families than war, but the kind of feckless righteousness that really believes laws and preachments can make liquor disappear. Add to that the millions of little acts of irrational contradiction that flourish between the two extremes and you will surely become as convinced as I am that we are all nuts. More than one kind of intoxication is involved in the conflict, from hoping to get plastered in a bar to hoping to get one's name plastered on the pillars of righteous sobriety. All to no avail. No matter how hard the pious opposition to distilling alcohol has labored down through the centuries, humans have just kept right on making the stuff. If brickbats contained sugar, someone would have made whiskey out of them by now.

The absurdities in the battle to suppress drinking are endless. Even after all these centuries of unsuccessful war on distilled spirits, the word "liquor", still makes some people cringe, just as the word, "sex", does. It is proper enough to say that you have been to the village tavern, but not the corner bar. Hypocrisy is the name of the game.

During Prohibition and still true in some social circles, it was okay to drink alcohol for medicinal purposes but not simply to make you feel better. There were and are a whole lot more eye-fluttering euphemisms for getting drunk than for staying sober, as Benjamin Franklin once observed. There are preachers who condemn drunkards out of one side of their mouths and imbibe out of the other side. Monks in search of everlasting life invented fine liqueurs which shows that we are not all crazy all the time. When I was a child, our neighbors condemned my father for drinking beer while they made and drank more potent applejack. Mom thought it was okay for Dad to have a beer or two in the evening, but oh my, not the equivalent amount of alcohol in whiskey. Getting verbally eloquent on California's most expensive wines is now a mark of advanced civilization; getting mildly high on the cheap stuff from Concord grapes in Ohio is embarrassingly boorish. When I got interested, years ago, in making ethanol to fuel my tractor, the permit gang said that was fine so long as I did not drink one drop of it myself. Tractors have more rights than humans in the gimlet eyes of the Alcohol and Tobacco, Tax and Trade Bureau, or TTB (formerly the Bureau of Alcohol, Tobacco and Firearms). I once suggested to state authorities that they should allow corn farmers to make bourbon and sell it to wholesalers just like dairy farmers produced and sold milk. The reaction was like I had suggested turning haymows into legal brothels.

Fortunately, the desire to stop people from enjoying a good homemade drink is diminishing. Even the giant distilleries aren't as opposed to home distillation as they once were because they see how they can benefit financially from the rise in small, local distilleries just as big breweries learned to benefit from locally brewed craft beers. But the fossil remains of Prohibition still linger in our legal system because drunkenness really is a problem and some rules and regulations are needed. History once more repeats itself: the last shelter of obsolescence is the law-making bureaucracy itself.

So now comes this book by Victoria Redhed Miller, *Craft Distill-*

ing: Making Liquor Legally at Home that finally, finally, finally shines some sanity on the controversy and does it with sprightly good humor that is fun to read. She presents detailed information on the ins and outs of the wacky permit situation and how to find your way through it all. Rather than just being critical, she goes on to present positive suggestions in favor of granting more affordable permits to distillers who only want to make enough booze for home and personal use. Who knows but what those mighty minions in the TTB might listen this time and agree that making a little liquor at home encourages more jobs and money than trying to tax it into oblivion, as author Miller argues. There is precedent. The biblical Jesus turned water into wine without rendering Caesar a single penny, so why should turning wine into brandy for your daughter's wedding be a problem?

But author and distiller Miller (her middle name really is Redhed) makes of her book much more than just a plea for common sense in the world of distilled spirits. The author also provides the clearest and most detailed information on the home distillation process that I have read to date. (A whole lot more detailed than my book, I cringe to say.) Then she moves through the how-to of every kind of unholy spirits ever imagined including a tequila-like drink distilled from Jerusalem artichokes.

She also includes information about how to get permitted to make ethanol fuel. Even though in my opinion the ethanol industry is causing more environmental harm than it does good and is not sustainable, I think small, on-farm production of ethanol might have some merit. I know from experience that if you go to your local TTB office, you won't get much help. At present what we have here is just one more amazing distillation contradiction. To guarantee survival of the huge industry that makes ethanol for piston engines to drink, the government hands out millions of dollars in subsidies to farmers and distillers. But if you want to make a little liquor just for your own home consumption, you, by heaven, must pay.

Lastly, author Miller includes lots of practical information about all the flavorings and additives that are so much a part now of making distilled spirits more interesting and enjoyable. The age of artisanal foods has arrived and artisanal drinks too. Cheers to this ground-breaking new book.

— Gene Logsdon,
author of *Good Spirits:*
A New Look at Ol' Demon Alcohol

The Accidental Activist

Craft Distilling is written for anyone who is interested in the fascinating hobby and art of distilling liquor. Specifically, it is aimed at those who want to make really good-quality spirits, not just cheap or fast booze. Finally, *Craft Distilling* makes the case for pursuing this hobby legally, with emphasis on the United States and Canada.

Most of the current laws around distillery licensing and taxes in America date back at least to the repeal of Prohibition in 1933; some go back as far as the Civil War in the 1860s. A lot has changed since then. Since 1978, in the US we have been allowed to make large quantities of beer and wine at home with no licensing or oversight at all. The government says there are two issues that make distilled liquor production different: safety concerns and tax revenues. I will be addressing both these issues in detail in *Craft Distilling*.

In addition, I propose a solution that makes it possible for hobby distillers to pursue their craft legally, while effectively addressing the concerns of the government. It's clear that the system as it is today is unfair to people like me, who want to make liquor legally but not commercially.

We ought to be having fun with this! Part of my dream is to see the "craft" back in craft distilling. This means, among other things, embracing small-scale distilling at home. There is a lot of history to back up the importance of home distillation as part of a healthy economy. I hope you will ask yourself honestly why you are interested in distilling; "because I can get away with it" or "because it's easier" shouldn't be the reasons to make liquor illegally. Read on: I think you'll agree that there's a lot to be said for making liquor legally at home.

Cheers!

Why Make Your Own Liquor?

In 2014, I did presentations at three Mother Earth News Fairs (Washington, Pennsylvania and Kansas) on distilling liquor. At every one of those well-attended talks, people came up to me afterward and asked, "How come I can make all the beer and wine I want at home, but I can't legally make distilled spirits?"

A very good question. My own adventures in the licensing process, detailed in chapter 3, led me to the interesting conclusion that there really is no good reason not to allow limited home distillation of liquor. Many people are very surprised to learn that it is, in fact, illegal in this country (and most of the world) to distill liquor without a license. The penalties, which are ridiculous in light of the fact that we can legally make beer and wine, are as outdated as the laws themselves; so harsh, you would think no one would dare attempt to make their own liquor for fear of being caught.

So why is home or hobby distilling so popular, and growing so fast? We don't have a television here at our off-grid homestead, so I'm quite out of the loop with what's out there in TV land, but I do hear things. Friends have enthusiastically told me about a show called *Moonshiners*. Chances are if you're reading this book, you've heard of the show. One fan of *Moonshiners* said he'd like to set up his own still. "Doesn't look all that hard," he said. Not having seen the show myself, I'm not sure what kind of still they use or what kind of liquor they make, but I do know from experience that in some senses it's true it's not all that hard. To me, though, in some ways it's almost impossibly complex and subjective. Kind of like *The Naked Chef* meets *Bill Nye the Science Guy*. Maybe not.

I'm just guessing here, but I suspect that many people who think of taking up distilling as a hobby do so because they think it will save them money to make their own. Probably they (like me) already have experience making beer and/or wine at home, which can quite often save you a lot of money. And it's true that the same mashing and fermenting equipment you have for beer and wine-making can be used for part of the booze-making process. However, once you start adding up the cost of the actual distilling equipment (figure several hundred dollars on up for a new, decent-quality, hobby-sized still), those potential savings seem to dry up rapidly.

Then there's the time involved. When you make beer, most of the time, you have something ready to drink in a week or two. With distilled spirits, you start by mashing and fermenting grain just like for beer, but then you're going to be distilling that liquid at least twice, and each time the volume of liquid decreases as the alcohol becomes more concentrated. If you're making something like whiskey, you'll want to age it for a while, so that's more time.

That said, you might be surprised to learn that the commercial distilling industry, as we know it today, has its roots in the kitchens and outdoor distilleries of homesteads, small farms and rural villages. Terms like "moonshine," which always seem to connote illegal distilling, and other somewhat derogatory names for homemade liquor, have left the general public with the idea that somehow home distilling is something to be ashamed of and kept strictly secret. Oh, how I would like to see that misleading image changed.

If you happen to live on a farm or homestead that has been in your family for at least a hundred years, chances are, at some point, one tenant or another turned to making and selling liquor when times were tough. Many a small farm kept going, albeit in straitened circumstances, when the resident distiller gained a reputation for producing the best whiskey or corn likker in the county.

The Original Farm Enterprise

Homesteaders bartered for just about everything they couldn't grow or hunt or make, but they needed cash to pay their property taxes. Distilling liquor, usually whiskey, provided a cash "crop" that, in many cases, was the difference between keeping their land and losing it. Farmers who had emigrated from Europe tended to be suspicious of the local water supply, so they made and drank beer, hard cider and distilled spirits instead.

After the Whiskey Rebellion in the 1790s (more on this in chapter 2), farmers moved west and learned to grow corn. Roads to the East Coast markets were unreliable, and if the trip took too long, the precious cargo of grain would rot en route. They soon discovered that there was a steady and lucrative market for corn whiskey, so the corn that wasn't converted to pork was converted to whiskey. It had the advantage of being able to survive the long trip east, regardless of weather or the time involved. And of course, it was also a much more profitable way to market the corn.

In his book *Good Spirits: A New Look at Ol' Demon Alcohol*, Gene Logsdon says that the Appalachia region would still be a prosperous area today if the post-Prohibition destruction of thousands of home stills hadn't taken place (at great taxpayer expense). It makes sense when you realize that, for many homesteaders living through the Depression, selling distilled liquor was often their only means of raising the cash to pay their property taxes and keep their farms.

In pioneer households, as in rural parts of England as recently as the late 1800s, it often was the duty of the woman of the house to make the beer, hard cider and distilled liquor. The men, naturally, had really important things to do like killing something for dinner. Home management books of the mid to late 1800s often include recipes and techniques for distilling and brewing. Large estates usually had a stillroom in the main house, used for concocting alcohol-based herbal tinctures and other remedies, as well as cordials and liqueurs.

The fact is, home production of liquor, especially distilled spirits, was what you might call the original farm enterprise. Born of necessity on homesteads where creativity and hard work meant the difference between survival and failure, settlers and immigrants found a way to convert local grains and fruits into products with almost unlimited sales potential. In those days, when life was hard and every moment of pleasure was to be savored, men and women consumed a lot more alcoholic beverages, on average, than we do today. So whether it was rye whiskey in New York or bourbon in Kentucky, home distillers found a ready market for their spirits as equipment and skills evolved and improved.

Virtually any distilled spirit you can name is essentially an agricultural product, fermented and distilled from fruits, grains, sugar cane and myriad herbs and spices. Here in Washington State, a wide variety of terrain and climate types make it possible to grow an astounding range of grains, fruits and vegetables. In the cool, moist maritime climate west of the Cascade Mountains, apple orchards abound, and some grains also do well. I had no idea until recently that quite a lot of corn is cultivated north of Seattle. East of the Cascades, the rolling hills and warmer, drier climate are ideal for growing cherries and other tree fruit, wheat and wine grapes.

One of the interesting conditions of having a distiller's license in Washington is that at least 50 percent of the raw materials used must come from Washington. Personally I think this is a great idea. It's good for Washington farmers who supply the ingredients like wheat or barley, and the distillers get those ingredients at a better price because they can be bought in season, and cost isn't tacked on to compensate for shipping expenses.

You might decide to pursue distilling as a hobby. All well and good. But do put some thought into what your motivation is for doing so. Maybe you don't need to sell moonshine to keep from losing your land, but there are plenty of ways small-scale distilling can fit nicely into a more self-reliant lifestyle. If I have my way, before too long more states will have a law like New York's Farm Distillery Act (more about this in chapter 24), and it will be that much easier for farms to have their own distilleries. In the meantime, though, those of us who don't want to make liquor as a business are having a tough go of finding a way to do so legally. More on this later.

Won't People Just Drink More
If They Make Their Own Spirits?

Let's get this out of the way right now. I realize I'm not going to be able to convince everyone that making your own liquor doesn't necessarily mean you'll drink more. My own experience, and I daresay most people who make their own beer and wine will say the same, is that I give away more of the beer and wine I make than I ever drink myself. If you've ever given away a jar of homemade jam, or handpainted a greeting card or baked a loaf of bread to surprise someone, you'll know what I mean. There is no small satisfaction in creating something beautiful or delicious and then sharing it with someone else. Once you go through the process, and see what it takes in time and effort to produce even one bottle of quality spirits, you will be justly proud of your accomplishment. Don't take my word for it; try it for yourself.

I know I harp on history in this book, but there is a lot to be learned from it in the case of liquor production and home distillation.

A Revenooer Walked into
a Nanaimo Bar...

*Home fermentation and distillation of spirits
has been a case study in the repression of human rights
from the very beginning of U.S. history.*

[Gene Logsdon, *Good Spirits: A New Look at Ol' Demon Alcohol*]

It occurs to me that a brief look at the history of distilling and liquor taxes would be useful here, to give context to my position on allowing limited home distillation of spirits. Some of this may come as a surprise to you; it certainly was an eye-opener for me. In fact, if I hadn't gone into the backstory of all this, in the course of researching this book, I doubt I would have been motivated to propose a change in the laws regarding distillation.

Remember the Boston Tea Party of 1773? That happened because the colonists were miffed about the British tax on tea, or so we've all been taught. True, they were unhappy about the tea tax, but it was the Molasses Act, a tax on rum, that really had them so upset. In those days, the production and sale of rum were critical to the colonial economy. Molasses was imported through traders from Jamaica and distilled into rum all over New England. The rum was then traded for slaves in Africa, and the slaves were traded for more molasses. Naturally, the traders reaped profits on each transaction.

Although the colonists produced and consumed vast quantities of beer and hard cider, there was a constant demand for rum. So when the British tried to stick their fingers in the profitable molasses pie, the colonists reacted by dumping a whole lot of tea into the harbor. (I expect they warmed up for this exciting event by fortifying themselves first with a few shots of rum at the local tavern.) Apparently at least one of them stayed just sober enough to realize what a waste it would be to dump perfectly good rum.

One of the most striking things I discovered is that, at least as far back as the Revolutionary War, taxes on alcohol have consistently been raised (or new ones imposed) to pay for wars. A huge debt weighed down the government following the Revolutionary War, over $2 billion in 1790s dollars. Secretary of the Treasury Alexander Hamilton, along with George Washington (who was himself a whiskey distiller), had the bright idea of imposing a stiff tax on liquor to raise funds. What really angered the colonists was that Hamilton demanded the tax be paid in cash.

The problem was that, at the time, no one had any cash. Small farmers and homesteaders, skilled distillers that they were, kept their farms afloat (and sometimes even profitable) by selling whiskey. They also used whiskey in lieu of cash, recognizing that whiskey was something nearly everyone wanted. So for many of them, this new tax would effectively ruin their chances to keep their land, much less make a profit from it. As far as they were concerned, it was even worse than the imposition of the Molasses Act by the British. Is it any wonder they rebelled?

The liquor taxes stayed in place until they were abolished by our third president, Thomas Jefferson. He apparently realized that the taxes were an unfair burden on homesteaders and farmers who depended on the sale of moonshine and whiskey. The taxes were reinstated for several years around the time of the War of 1812. After the war debts were settled, the taxes were lifted once again. There followed nearly 50 years of relative peace for the cash-strapped settlers; they could make beer, hard cider and liquor all day long with no worries about disgruntled neighbors turning them in or government busybodies showing up with their hands out.

In the wake of the Whiskey Rebellion (put down violently by George Washington and a ridiculous number of his troops), many of the Scots and Irish living in Pennsylvania at the time moved west, in hopes of making a new life for themselves in more tolerant surroundings. In Kentucky they found natural limestone water and fertile land ideal for cultivating corn. Having brought their stills and skills with them, they soon learned to make whiskey using mostly corn in place of the rye and other grains they were used to.

Since nearly everyone wanted liquor of some kind, the relocated settlers had no trouble selling their whiskey. In addition, they soon discovered that, once mashed, the corn and other grains made an excellent feed for hogs. So whiskey was not only a value-added product, but also part of a minimal-waste permaculture system.

Abraham Lincoln (who, by the way, opened a saloon in Illinois in 1833 where he served up a variety of domestic and foreign spirits in addition to the local wines, cider and beer) brought back liquor taxes in 1862, to help pay for the Civil War. Ironically, this act (quite predictably) resulted in such a price increase that it actually prompted the beginning of the bootlegging business, resulting in a decline in the sales of legal liquor, and thus a decline in tax revenues.

Prohibition, ushered in by the Eighteenth Amendment in 1919, was a complete disaster. It has been estimated that, by the time of its repeal in 1933, Prohibition had cost the government $11 billion in lost tax revenues; that's in 1930s dollars. Then there were all the state and local taxes lost, and the cost of nearly useless attempts at enforcement.

To me, the most infuriating loss of the Prohibition years was the income lost to thousands of farmers, who had previously sold their grain and fruit to distilleries, but now had nowhere to sell their crops. Many more small farmers lost their farms and ended up on welfare, simply because they could no longer earn their way by selling liquor. By the time of the presidential election of 1932, economists and government officials generally admitted that Prohibition was a prime cause of the Great Depression. Franklin D. Roosevelt won the election in a landslide victory, largely on the strength of his promise to repeal Prohibition.

Stop Calling It a "Sin" Tax

I'm really trying to avoid using the word "hypocrite" when referring to the government's position on liquor taxes, but honestly! Why are they still calling liquor tax a "sin" tax? If it's so sinful, you'd think the government would run, and run fast. But no, they are just as greedy for those tax dollars as ever, and I guess they're hoping no one will notice a small double standard. Think about it: Most of the famous liqueurs in the world are produced by monks, or at least their recipes originally came from monasteries. Wine has been used in church rituals for thousands of years. Dom Perignon, for heaven's sake!

And not to be a pedant, but isn't calling liquor a "sin" violating the separation of church and state?

We sure seem to have a wishy-washy relationship with booze in our culture. Everyone, or just about everyone, wants it, but we've been conditioned to act as if somehow that isn't true. Why is it a sin?

The Bible doesn't say drinking alcohol is a sin; true, drunkenness is frowned on, but that's not the same thing, is it? If what the government means is that they think it's bad for us to drink at all (did I mention hypocrisy?), then they should just say so. They will, of course, then be painting themselves into a corner. If you tax liquor because it's unhealthy, then by golly, we should be taxing soda pop and extra cheese on our pizza and that extra spoonful of sugar we snuck into our coffee when no one was looking.

Personally, I like a drink or two in the evening. I mean, geez, I'm a writer, people *expect* me to drink, you know. I like beer; I like port; I like Irish whiskey. I like trying new cocktails occasionally. And, I like to drink in moderation, which is just as well considering Washington State's liquor taxes. It's not a sin, people. Come on! It's FUN!

The truth is, whenever regulations and taxes have been relaxed on the production of alcohol, the result has been economic benefit for everyone: the government, consumers and the liquor industry as well. For example, look at what happened when Americans were first allowed to make beer and wine at home in 1978. They started making beer and wine, and got better and better at it. They formed clubs, organized competitions and kept on learning and practicing their craft. Some took the next step and licensed the first microbreweries and farm wineries. Along the way, jobs were created, permit fees and sales taxes were collected, and consumers enthusiastically embraced these unique, top-quality, locally produced products.

To all intents and purposes, the liquor tax structure in the United States has remained the same since the Civil War. Liquor is such a convenient thing to tax, simply because consumption is nearly universal. The government likes to call liquor tax a "sin" tax, no doubt to justify continuing to raise these taxes, which, by the way, clearly favor the rich.

The fact is, unfairly high taxes on liquor actually encourage the mass production of cheap, low-quality spirits! In chapter 25, I offer my proposal for allowing limited home production of distilled liquor. Far from depriving the government of those coveted tax dollars, I'll show you how going back to allowing distillation of liquor as a hobby or as a farm enterprise will, in fact, ultimately benefit the economy.

CHAPTER
3

100% PURE GRAIN SPIRIT

Making Liquor Legally
at Home

All I wanted was to make some booze.

I had been making beer and wine, champagne and port for years, and I'd often wondered about how distilled liquor was made. It seems silly now, but at the time, I assumed it was a complicated, mysterious process, simply because a bottle of whiskey was so much more expensive than a bottle of beer. Plus, in Washington State, you could buy beer and wine at a grocery store, but "hard" liquor was only to be purchased at a state-run liquor store.

Long before we moved to the farm in 2006, I bought a copy of *Making Pure Corn Whiskey* (see Books in Appendix A) at the local homebrew supply shop. It was fascinating reading, but honestly, I got bogged down in what seemed unbelievably complicated and "scientific" to me at the time. I can't remember how I first learned that distilling liquor without a license is illegal in most countries. I do remember wondering why I was allowed to make relatively huge amounts of beer and wine as a hobby, with no one inspecting my kitchen or caring how fabulous or skunky my beer tasted. Why was making distilled liquor so different?

Back in 2008, the Washington State Liquor Control Board created a new distilling license called the Craft Distillery license. This license, which came into being largely due to the efforts of Don Poffenroth and Kent Fleishman of Dry Fly Distilling in Spokane, WA, is a much less expensive option for smaller-scale distillers in our state. At this writing, it allows annual production of up to 150,000 proof *gallons* of distilled liquor; a proof gallon is defined as a US gallon at 50% ABV (alcohol by volume), at 20°C/68°F. That is a lot of booze. It's even more once it's diluted to drinking strength.

In June 2012, the 139 state-run liquor stores in Washington closed after legislation promoting the privatization of liquor sales passed easily. Costco, a major sponsor of the bill, spent over $21 million to convince voters that eliminating the "monopoly" of state-run liquor stores would result in greater availability and better selection. (Incidentally, liquor sales in the state are now controlled almost entirely by two huge distributors; I have a hard time considering what amounts to a duopoly as much of an improvement.)

We don't have a television here, so other than second-hand reports from friends, we missed out on all the 30-second soundbites of the vote-for-privatization media blitz (boo hoo). I actually read the entire initiative. Guess what: When I looked at the financial part of the fine print, it seemed to me that the cost of liquor would actually go up, not down. Why? Well, there is the state excise tax on liquor (20.5 percent, at this writing, by far the highest in the country), the additional "liter" tax ($3.77 per liter) and taxes paid by distributors and retailers. Oh and the kicker: the retail markup.

For example, at the state liquor stores, we were buying our favorite (at the time) Irish whiskey for about $23 per bottle. At one of the new local retail sources, suddenly the same bottle cost about $36. I like the stuff, but not that much. We simply quit buying it.

To me, it was no surprise that, in the months after the state liquor stores closed, applications for the Craft Distillery license began to be submitted at a rapid rate. Prior to June 2012, there were about 35 licensed distilleries in the state. Washington is now home to over 110 craft distilleries, accounting for about 25 percent of all craft distilleries in the country!

The commercial distillery business is booming here, helped along by an abundance of locally grown grains, fruits and herbs, and a consumer base eager to buy the premium spirits being produced. So what about people like me, who are interested in distilling as a hobby rather than as a business?

Cooler Heads Prevail in New Zealand: A Case Study

History clearly shows that there is a point of diminishing returns when it comes to taxing liquor. Higher taxes naturally mean higher prices, and higher prices only encourage more people to buy less and turn to making their own clandestine spirits. You may have heard of the notorious illegal "gin mills," which flourished by the thousands in London through most of the 19th century; nearly everyone wanted gin, but with more and more taxes, the working classes and the poor couldn't afford to buy it legally. In Scotland, after the first excise taxes were slapped on Scotch whiskey in the late 1700s, illegal stills popped up everywhere; at one point, there were an estimated 400 illegal stills, and only 8 legal distilleries, in Edinburgh alone. I heard a more recent story of someone who distilled an entire case of Budweiser beer, the result being about eight ounces of supposedly drinkable "gin."

Of course, at least some of the taxes collected on legal sales of spirits end up being used in a usually futile attempt to police the evil moonshiners. I know learning from history is out of fashion these days, but about 20 years ago, the New Zealand government took a bold step forward when they did just that. (Full disclosure: I broke out into a Highland reel during Happy Hour when I heard this story. And no, there is no video on Facebook to prove it.)

Prior to 1996, home distilling was still illegal in New Zealand. Around that time, a bright and courageous government worker noticed something. Even when police were able to find and bring charges against illicit distillers, the maximum fine that could be imposed was $500. Well, this fellow knew that, on average, several thousand dollars was spent prosecuting each one of the poor boobs, who weren't even making all that much liquor. This doesn't make sense, he reasoned. It wasn't as if the home distillers were selling the stuff, thereby stealing tax dollars out of the hands of the government. Hmm, thought he, what if we simply allow them to make a small amount of distilled liquor, along with the beer and wine they were already making perfectly legally?

Presumably this enlightened soul had to run his idea past the powers that be, but the net result was positive on all sides. The law was simply amended so that "distilled spirits" was added to "beer and wine" on the list of what private individuals could produce in non-commercial quantities. The only real caveat was that they would not be allowed to sell their spirits, but they weren't doing that anyway. These were hobbyists who made spirits in small stills, in their spare time, and their output rarely exceeded an amount that could easily be enjoyed among the distiller and his enthusiastic friends and neighbors.

Freed from the necessity to waste resources on fairly useless enforcement efforts and prosecution, the government found it had more time and money to spend on better things. And contrary to the fears of some, the country did not suddenly descend into a culture of debauchery and economic mayhem.

The home distillers, freed from the necessity of pursuing their hobby in a secretive manner, began to form clubs and started online forums in which they shared their enthusiasm, skills and ideas with other like-minded individuals. Soon some of these distillers were pooling their resources, expanding their basement and garage distilling operations into licensed commercial (but still small-scale) craft distilleries. Jobs were created. The local economy benefited from tax revenues generated by those supplying ingredients to the distilleries. And of course the government benefited from the tax revenues generated by liquor sales, not to mention permit fees.

From Homebrew to Microbrewery

As mentioned in chapter 2, this is just what happened after home beer-making was legalized in the US in 1978. Home brewers, finally able to practice their craft openly, quickly started writing books and publishing magazines devoted to their craft. In addition to producing classic beer styles, craft brewers were soon concocting some new and interesting variations on old styles of beer. The hops industry grew, in order to meet the demand for more variety and quantity of hops, ditto the suppliers of barley and other grains used in brewing. Homebrew shops popped up, even in small towns, many started by homebrewers.

Next came the first microbreweries and brewpubs, and cities like Seattle became tourist destinations for the equally enthusiastic consumers of the new "microbrews." More jobs created, more revenues from taxes and permit fees, more money staying in the local economy. Oh and a whole lot of happy consumers, who didn't want necessarily to make beer themselves but were thrilled by the ever-expanding selection of locally produced beer. A whole world had opened up, a world where beer didn't have to come in a can.

And by the way, nearly 40 years later, this industry is still growing!

Why Bother with a License?

In late 2012, I applied for a Craft Distillery license. Many have asked why I bothered. We live in a fairly remote area, quite a distance from our nearest neighbors, with no through traffic nearby. The implication seemed to be that we could easily get away with running a still up here, so why not just do it and not bother applying for a license?

First, I had learned that, contrary to common perception, it is illegal to distill alcohol without a state license, and (in the United States) a federal permit as well. (Some recently published books and magazine articles erroneously suggest that it's not illegal if you're only making liquor for private consumption.) It's just a random quirk of my personality that I prefer to do things legally. Also, I had recently submitted a proposal package for my first book. Although I was still waiting to hear if it was accepted for publication, I was already mulling the idea of writing a book about distilling. In particular, I was thinking of writing about the licensing process; at that time, I could not find anything in print that explained the current licensing process in the United States.

I should mention that, when I applied for this license, I didn't know much of anything about distilling, and didn't own a still. I did start spending more time reading on the subject, and eventually began to think I was starting to understand the basic principles involved. I was particularly interested in the fact that, in addition to all the science involved, there is also quite a lot that is more subjective and up to the distiller to decide at various stages of the process, what might be called the "art" or "craft" of distilling.

As I navigated my way through the distillery licensing process, I discovered a few things. For example, the licensing process is completely biased toward commercial distillers. This seemed odd to me. I am not allowed to make distilled liquor without a license, but at the same time, the licensing process is, if anything, more difficult for someone like me. Could it really be true that I was the first person to apply for this license who wasn't planning to pursue it as a business? It seemed unlikely, yet it also seemed to be the case.

You might be amused to hear a few of the things that happened after I submitted my application. (Keep in mind that the authorities assumed that I was opening a commercial distillery.) About two weeks after mailing in my state application, I had a phone interview with not one but two Liquor Control Board representatives. I was asked why I wanted the license. Not having anticipated that question, I improvised: I said I was a writer and was researching a book. (Since I was still waiting to see if my first book was accepted by the publisher, it was a bit of a stretch to project as far as a possible second book.) I wanted to write about the licensing process, I went on glibly, so I thought I should go through the process so I can write about it intelligently.

Silence. I swear I could hear them scratching their heads, or maybe that was my heavy breathing. When they asked me how much I was going to produce and sell, I said I wasn't planning to sell anything. I just wanted to make a small amount to enjoy myself and share with my family and friends. More silence. Finally one of them said they'd have to check something and call me back.

I will say for them that they did, in fact, call me back the next day. "You can't get a distillery license," I was told, "unless you sell the liquor you make." Huh? This was my first inkling that something was not quite right in Dodge City. I mean, I was trying to do the right

Show Me Your Federal Permit, If You Live in Missouri

In October 2014, I did a presentation on distilling at the Mother Earth News Fair in Topeka, KS. A gentleman came up after the talk and asked if I was aware that it is legal to make up to 100 gallons of distilled liquor annually in Missouri. I was very surprised to hear this, although at the time I hadn't done extensive state-by-state research on the subject. Later I did look it up. It turns out that Missouri, which has always had some of the most lenient liquor-related laws in the country (it never went completely "dry" during Prohibition), allows anyone at least 21 years of age to make up to 200 gallons total of any kind of liquor, including distilled liquor, each year without a license. Well—learn something new every day.

Before you decide to pull up stakes and move to Missouri, it's important to note that, legally, Missourians will need to obtain a Federal Basic Permit if they are making distilled liquor. If I get my way (see my proposal in chapter 25), every state will adopt a similar model, and no one will need a federal permit provided they make less than a specified amount of booze and comply with state regulations. I am encouraged, actually, to learn that at least Missouri has seen the light.

thing! I knew I needed a license to distill booze legally, and that's what I wanted to do. And it turned out that they expected me to sell the stuff, *and* submit a sales report and any taxes collected, every single month. In other words, I could not be licensed to distill liquor as a hobby.

Still, I persevered. I was told to post a notice, printed on bright yellow paper, near my front door for several weeks (can't remember exactly how many days, at least 30 I think). It was to notify neighbors that we had applied for a distillery license and give them time to comment, just in case someone thought a distillery might adversely affect the "character of the neighborhood."

We got a good laugh out of that. First of all, our house is half a mile in from our gate. No one would see the notice if we put it by our front door, unless we invited them and unlocked the gate. Second, our nearest neighbor is two miles down the hill from us. Anyway, we decided to go with the spirit (no pun intended) of the law instead of the letter, and posted the notice on our gatepost. We figured that chances were very good that anyone who actually saw the notice would be all in favor of a distillery in the neighborhood; frankly, we thought if anything, it would improve the character of the neighborhood!

Distilling in Canada

Canada's first recorded distillery was licensed in Quebec City in 1769. By the 1840s, there were over 200 licensed distilleries in the country, almost all of them making whiskey. Today, the Canadian distilling industry produces a variety of spirits including rum, vodka, gin and liqueurs. Canadian whiskies are mainly blends and have a distinctive flavor, being distilled primarily from corn and rye.

Distillery licensing in Canada is handled within each province. For many years, Ontario had more whiskey distilleries than any other province, with a total of three. Recently, more smallish craft distilleries have been opening up in several provinces.

As in most of the world, distilling at home without a license is currently not permitted in Canada. See Appendix B for a summary of Canadian licensing regulations organized by province.

What's Next for Home Distillers?

In chapter 25, I will be discussing in more depth my reasons for believing it's time to change the laws to allow limited home production of distilled liquor. The government's stated concerns (safety issues and tax revenue issues) are, in my view, easily dealt with. I have developed a proposal for both the state licensing and federal permit processes that address government concerns while at the same time amending outdated laws to treat non-commercial distillers fairly.

In the meantime, read on. It's time to have some fun and learn about craft distilling!

The Basic Principles
of Distillation

Simply put, distillation is a physical process in which liquids are heated and their compounds then separated based on their different boiling points. There are many different compounds in a typical alcoholic wash. Some are poisonous; some contribute various esters and other elements that influence flavor. And of course there is the "good stuff," ethyl alcohol or ethanol. Some of the compounds have a lower boiling point than ethanol and others have a higher boiling point. The science of distillation involves understanding how to accurately separate the dangerous elements from the potable ethanol. The art and craft of distillation, at least in part, involves deciding how much of the various flavor-influencing elements to allow into the mix and then accurately controlling these factors.

It's important to realize that the distillation process does not *create* alcohol; it simply concentrates the alcohol content of a fermented wash by removing much of the water and other non-alcoholic elements. However, the process of distilling does greatly influence the final product by both creating flavors and selecting flavor compounds.

Of course, the various compounds in the still will all vaporize to one degree or another, so in principle, the separation of the compounds can never be perfect. Even commercial high-separation fractionating stills, designed to maximize the separation of the vapors as they rise through the column, cannot achieve complete separation of all the elements in the wash. That said, it is certainly possible, with a good understanding of the distillation process and quality distilling equipment, to get excellent results with small-scale distilling equipment. It's kind of like photography: Having great equipment is a good start, but results also depend on the skill and eye of the photographer.

List of Typical Compounds in Alcohol Wash, in Order of Boiling Point

Compound	°C	°F
Acetaldehyde	20.2	68.36
Propionaldehyde	49	120.2
Iso-butyraldehyde	62	143.6
Ethyl acetate	74	165.2
Ethyl alcohol	**78.3**	**172.94**
Isopropyl alcohol	83	181.4
Butylaldehyde	95	203
Propyl alcohol	97	206.6
Water	100	212

Although ethanol vaporizes at a much lower temperature (78.4°C/173.1°F) than water, some water will always be present in the distillate. This is because even before it gets to the point of boiling, water begins to vaporize. Watch your teakettle next time you're heating it up; it will be steaming merrily away well before it actually comes to a boil.

What's an Azeotrope?

An azeotrope occurs when two liquids with different boiling points form a liquid with a unique boiling point. In the case of ethanol and water, the azeotrope occurs at a mixture of 96.5% ethanol and 3.5% water; this mixture's boiling point is 78.15°C/172.67°F. In a practical sense, then, especially on a small scale, 96.5% ethanol is as close as you can get to pure ethanol, no matter how many times you distill. Commercially, for example in the production of fuel ethanol, special equipment makes it possible to produce pure ethanol.

This Explains Mom's Spaghetti Sauce

I remember, while growing up, seeing my mom add red wine to the pan when she was making spaghetti sauce. Neither of my parents drank alcohol, so if it occurred to me to think about it at all, I would wonder why Mom used wine for cooking. I do remember hearing someone explain vaguely that it was OK because the alcohol would "cook off" during the several hours that the sauce was simmering. So it wasn't the same as drinking the wine, you know.

Believe it or not, it wasn't until I started learning about distilling that I figured out how this works. Now I know that ethanol vaporizes at about 78°C/173°F, well below the boiling point of water. So when the stuff in the pot starts steaming, that steam contains a high percentage of alcohol. However, if the pot has a fairly tight lid, most of that steam will condense on the lid and drop right back into the pot! Still, Mom was probably right that at least a good share of the alcohol does cook off. And frankly, even if it doesn't, who cares? She still makes the best damn spaghetti sauce ever.

Building a Small Column Still

I really don't know what possessed me to think I could build my own still. It's probably one of those many things that I will do exactly once in my lifetime. I spent quite a bit of time learning to solder copper, and used a design that didn't seem all that complicated; no tricky angles or any of that kind of thing. It still took me a lot of time to put this thing together. Anyone who knows how to solder copper would have had it done in a weekend in time for Happy Hour on Sunday. Oh well.

There are lots of different types of stills, and many variations on each design. I chose to start with a simple column still. This was partly because I had learned enough to know that this kind of still was the best for making things like gin and vodka. Also, I had a book that had a detailed plan for building that kind of still.

The basic types of still to choose from on a hobby scale are pot stills and column or fractionating stills. Of the two, column stills are considered more efficient in terms of their ability to accurately separate the different compounds in the wash being distilled. This is the kind of still you'll probably choose if you're aiming to make decent gin or vodka, or even pure ethanol for fuel. It is capable of producing a very clean, neutral spirit.

Pot stills are the traditional type of still used for making whiskey. Their relative inefficiency is not entirely a liability; less complete separation of various compounds results in a spirit with more esters and other flavor elements left in. If you plan only to make flavor-positive liquor like whiskey or rum or perhaps brandy, a pot still may meet your needs.

Should you buy or build a still? This is another decision that only you can make. These days, a new hobby-sized copper pot still of good quality will probably cost several hundred dollars. If you have the spare time, some mechanical skills and a lot of patience, you can certainly build a good still that will produce top-quality spirits. Seriously, if I can manage a project like this, you could do it too. Depending on the design, you might or might not save significant money building your own, so think about it before you make a fast decision.

What kind of still should you make or buy? I sometimes feel like every time I answer a question, my reply starts with "Well, it depends." But there are so many factors that go into a choice like this: Price, size of still, type of liquor you want to make, local availability and more. Your best bet would be to ask for a recommendation from other small-scale distillers, or still manufacturers that cater to hobby distillers.

If you do decide to build your own still, be sure to use only lead-free solder. And do read through all the directions in the plans first, so you can be sure you understand the techniques, skills needed and the steps involved in the assembly process.

To build my still, I used the column still plan in Ian Smiley's book *Making Pure Corn Whiskey*, which I highly recommend. However, I made a few modifications to his basic design to fit my needs, as well as my skill level. First, his still design employs a smallish electric hot-water heater as the boiling pot. Assuming I would be using a propane burner to heat my still, I substituted my stainless steel stockpot for the boiling pot; it had the advantage of having a nice ball valve installed, so I had been using it for mashing grain for beer.

Also, I had trouble with the soldering of the Liebig condenser, a small condenser that further cools distillate as it drips from the still. The plans called for soldering a ⅜" ID (inside diameter) copper tube inside a shorter ½" ID copper tube, with the smaller tube ends protruding through holes drilled in caps on the ends of the ½" tube. It also required two ⅛" ID copper tubing pieces, about 2 inches long, to be soldered into small holes drilled in the side of the ½" tube.

I tried and I tried but just couldn't do the soldering such that the joints didn't leak water. Probably there is some trick to it that a more experienced do-it-yourselfer would know; trying to solder such small joints in fairly thin copper was, at the time, beyond my skills.

Eventually I did figure out a way to compensate for the lack of Liebig condenser. I turn down the heat just a bit once distillate starts to drip from the still. This allows the condenser water to remain cool; hence, the distillate as it emerges is also cool.

The column on my still is 45" tall. All the main parts, including the column, are 1¼" copper pipe. The column is packed with pure copper mesh, which is critical to the fractionating process that comes into play when distilling high-proof spirits or pure ethanol. At the top of the column, at the right-angle junction of the column and the still head, a laboratory thermometer (which measures up to 230°F) is strategically placed to continuously gauge the still head temperature. This

Here the condenser coil is partly pulled out of the condenser tube. Note the top of the condenser tube is open, which prevents pressure buildup.

The horizontal still head, and the condenser tube on the right.

The stainless-steel boiling pot, showing the ball valve drain and fitting for thermometer near the bottom.

temperature is an important guide when estimating how much alcohol is left in the still during a distillation run. It also indicates what distillation stage is in progress at any given time.

At the other end of the still head, another copper pipe connects at right angles to the still head pipe, facing upward. This is the condenser tube, which houses the condenser coil. It's important to note that the top of the condenser tube is intentionally open. If it were closed off, pressure could build up in the still, creating a risk of explosion. This is a very important concept to keep in mind if you plan to build your own still.

The shell-and-tube type of condenser is essentially a heat exchanger. Cooling water runs through the coil, condensing vapors as they circulate around the coil. In this case, the coil is made from ⅛" ID copper tubing; I found that wrapping it around a ¾" OD (outside diameter) steel pipe to make the coil gave me just the right diameter to fit well but not tightly inside the condenser pipe. Before putting the coil in the condenser tube, I stuffed the inside of the coil with pure copper mesh; this acts as a heat sink and improves the condensing action of the coil.

Why Is Copper Important in a Still?

Copper is the material of choice for building stills because of its high thermal conductivity, malleability and catalytic properties. The interaction of copper and wash removes sulfurous flavors and heightens delicate fruit and floral aromatics.

I replaced the leaky Liebig condenser with this plain copper tube.

The Liebig condenser on my still, with water tubing attached.

Vinyl tubing brings cooling water into the coil and directs the water away as it exits the condenser coil. (See more about condensers and the water supply in chapter 10.)

Incidentally, I like the fact that I can easily detach my boiling pot from the column of my still. All I have to do is unscrew the union attached to the lid, which connects to the column tube. Then I can lift the pot off the burner and easily empty and clean it. It also means

My 2-liter essential oil distiller.

that I can use a different pot on the burner if needed, for instance to mash grains.

If I had it to do again, I would definitely make the condenser tube from a larger-diameter copper pipe. To make a coil that fits inside 1¼" pipe, you really have to use very small-diameter tubing like the ⅛" tubing in my coil. The problem was that the output on my little water pump is for 5/16" tubing; I had to step it down to a smaller tube that would fit snugly on the ⅛" copper tube. I believe the cooling would be more effective and efficient if the condenser coil was the same size tubing as the pump tubing.

Overall, though, I am very happy with my still and idiotically pleased with myself for sticking with it until I got the thing put together. Oh, and cost: As I said, I already had the boiling pot, so most of my expenses were for copper pipe, copper tubing and fittings. The largest pipe and fittings are 1¼", and I must admit being surprised at how expensive some of the fittings were. In total, I spent around $150 (in early 2013) for the materials to build the still.

My Essential-oil Distiller

In addition to my copper column still, I also have a small Pyrex essential-oil distiller. Its boiling pot has a capacity of only two liters, and it wasn't cheap (around $300), but it works extremely well. I sometimes use it for distilling liquor, especially when I have a very small batch to distill; in these cases, I often feel it is a more efficient use of fuel compared to using the much larger column still. I do also use it for distilling essential oils!

Someday, I would like to build another still similar in design to this one, to use as a separate beer-stripping still; the column could be much shorter and the pipe of larger diameter. I'll have to figure out first, though, where to put the thing in my 8-foot-by-10-foot stillhouse. There's no way I'm going to get rid of my dart board.

My column still. It is tall enough that I had to dig a pit for the propane burner that fires it. The column is secured for safety.

Your "Home" Distillery

I must admit I have been a bit irritated by recently published books and even magazine articles advocating "home" distilling. I know I'm way too literal most of the time, but to me, "home distilling" is misleading. The fact is, United States federal law prohibits the use of a still for liquor production inside your home, even if you are a licensed distiller. These books and articles were encouraging readers to make small stills using a teakettle or even a pressure cooker, to be used on the kitchen stove.

As you've already learned, there are a few specific safety issues that are critically important to be aware of with distilling. You might be thinking that if you do this on a small scale in your kitchen, who will know? Yes, you might get away with it. You probably believe that you're taking all precautions and nothing bad could possibly happen. Whatever else I think about most of the laws around distilling, I do totally agree with the idea of not running a still inside a home. It is simply not worth the risk, and you may also run into problems with insurance (see sidebar).

When I first applied for my distillery license, I was surprised to get a phone call a couple of weeks later from our local fire inspector. Evidently the Liquor Control Board had forwarded notice of my application to him. He was very nice and explained that he wanted to come inspect my "facility." I explained to him that I didn't have a "facility;" I didn't even have a still yet. My plan (such as it was) was to build a small still and use it on a propane burner on my patio. This clearly stumped the poor man, who said he would need to check something and call me back.

When he phoned me the next day, he said apologetically that it would not work for me to set up my distillery the way I had described. It definitely needed to be in a separate building. (I was later told by the regional Liquor Board inspector that a lot of small distilleries were being set up in garages.) This news left me feeling even more discouraged. I had visions of county health inspectors giving me a long list of requirements like top-to-bottom stainless steel, tile floors and a lot more.

Much to my relief, I found out that, at least in our state, the requirements for the building are as follows: four walls, a roof and a door that locks. That's it! I started thinking about it and looking around our place to see if something fitting that description was available.

It didn't take me long to spy a shed I had built several years earlier for our pigs. I had a smaller house I had built for pigs, but it really only worked well when we had two pigs, and only when they

My little stillhouse, converted from a shed I originally built for, well, pigs.

were smaller. It was definitely too small for three pigs, at least when they got to over 100 pounds or so. The new shed, which is built on skids to be easily movable, is about 8 feet by 10 feet. Luckily it had a high enough roof that I can easily enter and move around in it; actually the sloping roof is about 8 feet high at the doorway. At the time the front was completely open, but I built double doors onto it and added a sturdy hasp and a heavy-duty padlock.

So what do you need in your little distillery besides a still? Well, you need some way to heat the still. Depending on your situation, you might use electric heat, a propane burner or even a wood fire. You'll need access to running water for the condenser, and the appropriate hoses or tubing to connect the water to the still. You'll need containers to collect the distillate from the still and more containers with lids to age and store your finished spirits. Let's see: oak chips, cubes or barrels if you're going to be aging spirits with oak. Filtering equipment if you're making vodka. Various herbs and spices if you're making gin or bitters or liqueurs.

If you're also going to be doing your mashing in your stillhouse, you'll need good storage for your grains to keep moisture and rodents out. Maybe a grain mill. If you've been making your own beer, you probably already have all the required fermenting equipment. (See below for a fairly complete list if you are starting from scratch.)

Yet another thing that's not discussed much: Make sure you have something to do in your stillhouse while you're distilling. There's not actually all that much hands-on time during a small-scale distilling run, and you will be keeping an eye on things for probably two to three hours. We don't have cell phone reception or wireless Internet at our place, which might be just as well; I daresay it would prove just as big a distraction in the stillhouse as it is elsewhere. I usually bring at least one book, my MP3 player and headphones, and a notebook and pen.

I also have a dartboard in the stillhouse; turns out that if I stand just outside the threshold on the long door side, I'm almost exactly at the regulation distance from the board. If it sounds silly, I challenge you to try it. It's a lot of fun. Just make sure it's placed so you're not tripping over your still in the process of retrieving the darts from the ceiling.

Now you know what I do when I'm waiting for the still to come to a boil.

The Well-equipped Home Distillery

Besides the obvious still, there are quite a few things you should have on hand if your aim is to make really top-quality spirits. Don't let this list frighten you; you don't necessarily need to buy everything all at once. Eventually, though, if you are milling and mashing your own grains, you will find that most of this equipment will come in very handy.

Most of it can be found at homebrew and wine-making supply shops. If you're just starting out, do try to find a local shop; relatively large things like buckets can get a bit expensive to ship.

Mashing

- Grain mill (optional but nice)
- Mashing pot with lid (size depends on how much grain you will be mashing in a given batch; I use my stainless steel 10-gallon (38-liter) stockpot, as it is of ample size to handle 15 pounds (6.8 kg) or more of grain at one time)
- Large plastic, stainless steel or wooden spoon for stirring
- Accurate thermometer

I keep all my distilling grains in food-grade buckets with tight-fitting lids.

- Kitchen scale capable of weighing at least 10 pounds (4.5 kg) at a time
- Large food-grade buckets with tight lids for storing grain
- pH meter or pH test strips (I recommend investing in a pH meter if you are going to be doing a lot of this kind of thing; it's absolutely worth it.)
- Tincture of iodine (for testing mash for starch conversion)
- Immersion chiller (optional)

Fermenting

- At least 2 fermenting buckets with lids; a good size is 25 liters, about 6.6 US gallons
- Airlocks
- Good airtight storage for yeast and enzymes
- Hydrometer and test cylinder
- Siphon for transferring wort to the still

Distilling

- Heat source for heating the still
- Water supply for the condenser, and some means of reusing or disposing of the water (see the discussion on water in chapter 10)
- Graduated cylinders for collecting distillate. You can use other kinds of containers, but I find it very handy to use graduated cylinders. I have a 1-cup (250-milliliter [ml]) cylinder that collects the distillate as it comes from the still, and a 2-cup (500-ml) one that I dump the smaller one into when it fills up. I like to keep track as I go along, especially when doing a spirit run.
- Jars or bottles, with lids, for storing low wines, heads and tails, and finished spirits

Your Home Distillery and Insurance

Be sure to check your homeowner's insurance. Your policy may not cover things like exploding stills or fires in your stillhouse. Be sure to follow all local fire safety regulations. Locate your still in the approved kind of building, have the appropriate type of fire extinguisher handy to your still and don't allow anyone to smoke in the vicinity, especially when you are running the still. And always remember to lock those doors securely when you're not around!

The alcohol refractometer, a very handy tool for distilling.

- Approved fire extinguisher (check with your local fire department for the specific type needed)
- Alcohol refractometer. Not absolutely necessary, but it makes it so easy to check the ABV of distillate, particularly handy when you are doing spirit runs. Make sure you ask for an alcohol refractometer, as there are different types of this instrument, such as the Brix type. Do try to find a good-quality one.
- Hoses and other equipment for flushing and cleaning your still
- A notebook for record keeping. I am pretty sure you will regret it if you don't. I always think I'm going to remember from one batch to the next what exactly I did, but almost every time I have been wrong. I know I harp on this, but it's a good habit to get into.

The Economics of Distilling Your Own Liquor

It is interesting to me to note that, in all the distilling books I have recently seen, only one brings up the subject of economics. That one is specifically aimed at the commercial distilling industry, not hobby distillers. To me, though, it is critical to examine the numbers involved, since this relates directly to why the government says it doesn't want to allow home distillation of spirits.

When the state liquor stores closed in Washington, in June 2012, many residents believed that the cost of liquor would go down. This perception was understandable. The major sponsors of the bill led voters to believe that getting rid of the "monopoly" of state-run liquor stores would not only result in lower prices (presumably by increasing competition), but would also enhance selection and availability, by increasing the number of retail locations where consumers could buy liquor. It's true that there are now roughly 1,400 stores statewide that sell liquor (compared with the previous 139 state-run liquor stores). However, we have had an increasingly hard time finding some of our favorite brands in stores near us. I suspect that many of these stores—for example, our local Walgreen's Pharmacy—have relatively little shelf space to devote to liquor, so they have to limit their selection to a few of the more popular types. It makes sense, but it's still frustrating.

So why have Washington State's liquor prices gone up so much? As I mentioned before, Washington has the highest liquor taxes in the country; at this writing, the excise tax is 20.5%. There is also the "liter tax" of US$3.77 per liter, so that adds close to $3.00 for every 750-ml bottle purchased. (If these numbers seem outrageous, please note that Washington, at this writing, has no state income tax, although it has been recently proposed.) And although there are new annual fees collected at both the distribution and retail levels, the single biggest difference in the new pricing structure is the retail markup. There is more than one kind of liquor that we have simply stopped buying, due to the dramatic price increase.

I have certainly wondered if the boom in Craft Distillery license applications since June 2012 is, in part, due to a reaction to this increase in prices. Which brings us to the question of whether it is actually less expensive to make your own distilled liquor. It's an important question, not just for the obvious reason of how it will affect your personal finances. Part of the reason the government doesn't want people making their own liquor without a license is they believe that if consumers make their own, they'll stop buying liquor and the state will lose a lot of liquor-related tax revenues.

In chapter 25, I will show, using numbers from my own experience, how the worries about lost tax revenues simply don't apply when there is a reasonable limit on the amount of liquor a home distiller can make. First, let's look at what it takes, in time as well as money, to produce even a relatively small amount of ready-to-drink liquor. I promise I'm not trying to discourage you. But just in case your motivation is saving money by making your own, I don't want to deceive you. Remember, I am focusing in this book on making good-quality spirits, not just cheap spirits.

A Blinders-off Look at the Economics of Home Distillation

I'll bet you a Gin & Tonic that most people who take up liquor distillation do so mainly because they imagine they will save money on booze. Ring a bell? I'll further bet that, aside from cost, a certain percentage of these distillers will soon give up the hobby, once they discover how much time is involved.

For example: Say you are making a 5-gallon batch of malt whiskey. You buy 15 pounds or so of malt (it's a lot cheaper to buy a 50-pound bag, but you're not ready to commit yourself that far) and a package of premeasured whiskey yeast. So far you've spent about $25; add tax and shipping cost if you mail-ordered. Oh and add a couple bucks if you had the homebrew shop crush the grain for you.

Now you mash the grain, which takes two to three hours. You strain the mash, let the wort cool, then add the yeast. Fermentation begins, and takes anywhere from a few days to two weeks, depending on conditions. You fire up your still, do a stripping run (another two to three hours) and let the still cool down overnight. You now have about two liters of low wines. You spend half an hour or so emptying and flushing out the still before the spirit run. You fire up the still again, and spend nearly two hours slowly and carefully doing the spirit run. You now have (if you've done a good job of separating the hearts) about 450 to 600 ml hearts at 65% ABV. You're tempted to drink the stuff then and there, but it smells a bit harsh and raw. You decide to age it a bit. You dilute it to 55% ABV, toast some oak chips and toss them into the jar.

Now you wait. At least a month. Maybe three or four months. You strain out the oak chips, measure the alcohol content and dilute it

I'm so glad I kept good records right from the beginning. One thing I discovered is that as I gained experience with distilling, my yields of potable spirits increased noticeably. Presumably this is because I was getting better at making the cuts, and possibly I am also doing a better job of mashing the grains. So keep at it, take notes and remember that practice makes perfect.

to 40% ABV. Now you have about 800 ml of whiskey ready to drink, a little more than a bottle's worth. And you've spent weeks doing it!

True, if you're fairly experienced, detail-oriented, have good equipment and are aiming for high-quality spirits, all that time and effort will be rewarded. If you're like me and up for the challenge, you will be raring to go after reading this summary of the process. Or you may decide that it's not worth all that much trouble. Depending on the kind and quantity of liquor you plan to make, and whether you are able to buy some of your ingredients in bulk or from local suppliers, you may save money.

What's Your Time Worth?

Don't ignore or discount the time factor. Although the actual hands-on time is not an awful lot on any given day, some parts of the process are time-sensitive, so you will need to plan your schedule to be available for the next step. I often find myself thinking ahead about when to start something fermenting, just to be sure I will be at home and ready to distill once fermentation is done.

Did I scare you off from even trying? I hope not! I do think it's better to have some idea up front, though, of what you're getting into. Remember this is a hobby, not a full-time occupation. Ask yourself why you want to make your own spirits. Are you a beer brewer looking for a new challenge? Maybe you're daydreaming about having your own commercial distillery someday; in this case, I strongly encourage you to start small. My still, although much smaller than a commercial model, operates on exactly the same principles and is capable of producing excellent spirits. Many brewpubs and microbreweries began life as a hobby in someone's basement or garage; why shouldn't the same be true of craft distilleries?

It reminds me of what I tell people about raising turkeys. I heard that snicker! If you think you're going to save money raising your own turkey for Thanksgiving, well, you won't. You'll be feeding that thing for months, using the most expensive high-protein feed, before you're ready for turkey sandwiches. Plus, commercially grown turkeys are so cheap these days! On the other hand, you will have a fresh, homegrown turkey, and you can be justly proud of the investment of time and effort that went into putting it on your table.

Likewise, when you make your own premium spirits, you may not save money, and yes, you will invest a lot of time before you have a bottle of something ready to drink. I'll bet you another Gin & Tonic that you're smiling right now, anticipating the moment; go on, admit it. Sure, you could run out to the store and buy something, but where's the fun in that?

If People Distill Their Own Liquor, Won't They Quit Buying It?

An important point here is that we still buy some of our liquor. In the course of researching this book, I daresay I have spent a lot more time, in an average month, distilling liquor than most hobbyists will realistically do. I don't have a job outside the homestead, so I have a lot more "spare" time than most people. Even so, I'm not running the still more than a couple of times a week at the most. I would have to be fermenting at least three batches of something at any given time to have something ready to distill more often than that! You'd be surprised how quickly your kitchen floor can get crowded with fermenting buckets, and while it gives you a good excuse to put off mopping the floor, it does tend to induce muffled swearing when someone (OK, me) trips over a bucket on a late-night foraging excursion.

I have also been experimenting with a lot of different kinds of spirits. I have yet to come up with a reasonable facsimile of 18-year-old Glenlivet, and while we don't drink Scotch all that often, we do still buy it. I like my homemade genever-style gin for G & Ts, but David prefers a gin with less botanical character to it, so he buys Bellringer or some other brand. With all the kinds of whiskey I've tried making, I haven't yet made something akin to blended Canadian whiskey, so we still buy that.

I could go on, but you get the point. It's also important to realize that the size of your still (that is, its boiling pot capacity)

How Much Liquor Will a Bucket of Mash Yield?

Among all the distilling-related books I've read lately, not much seems to be written about yields. It seems to me that most would-be hobby distillers would want to at least have an idea of how much booze they will end up with after all that time and effort.

At this point in my limited experience, I believe that it's probably impossible to accurately predict consistent yields. Why? Well, there are a lot of variables involved, and actual yields depend on the skill of the distiller. For example, I know my mashing skills have improved over time. I'm doing a better job of controlling the mash temperature, resulting in more efficient mashing, which means more fermentable sugars in the mash. More sugar means more potential alcohol.

However, high-alcohol potential may not mean much if you don't do a good job of fermentation. Incomplete fermentation means wasted sugar and less alcohol in the wash. Remember, distilling doesn't create alcohol; it merely concentrates the alcohol by separating it from water and other compounds in the still. Your yields will also be influenced by your accuracy in making the cuts (more about this in chapter 10) during the distilling process.

I can honestly report that my yields have increased gradually, as I have gained knowledge, skill and experience. I know this because I have kept detailed notes of every single batch I have ever mashed, fermented and distilled.

So practice your craft. It will take time, yes, but your yields will improve. Chapter 9 contains a formula for calculating estimated alcohol in the wash before distilling; Chapter 10 includes a formula for calculating how much ethanol at 100% ABV is in your low wines after the first distilling run. This helps you estimate how much potable alcohol you will have after the second distillation. Don't skip ahead here; take your time, go through the process in order. Each step, from mashing to fermentation to distillation, will influence the ultimate yield from that bag of grain.

automatically limits the amount of liquor you can make. I promise this is true. You might think that you can just turn up the heat and run everything faster, but this is actually counter-productive, and can even be dangerous. Running it faster just puts more strain on your condenser (see the discussion on this in chapter 10), which can decrease yields. It's also much harder, with small quantities like this, to accurately make the "cuts" that separate the poisonous and undesirable elements from the potable ethanol in your still. Once again, I'm encouraging you to pursue this hobby with the goal of producing high-quality spirits, not cheap, quick rotgut.

Keep in mind that, depending on your location, you may or may not have a nearby source of equipment, ingredients and supplies. Do try to buy your stuff locally when you can. I know it's easy to just order everything online now, but consider the additional cost of shipping, all that extra packaging and those horrible peanut things to get rid of somehow. By the way, because home distilling is currently illegal, no one at the homebrew shop is allowed to answer questions or give you advice about distilling. No matter that they sell distilling yeast and even small counter-top stills (labeled carefully as being for water or essential oil distillation). Trust me, they are required to report sales of stills, even Internet sales, so proceed with caution if you haven't already applied for your license.

Mashing Grains

Mashing is the process in which starches are converted to fermentable sugars. Grains are mostly starch, protein and fiber; all grains are roughly 50 percent starch. For fermentation to work, starches must be broken down into simple sugars to enable the yeast to consume them. During mashing, the diastatic enzymes activated during malting (see sidebar What Is Malt?) go to work on the starches.

Starches consist of long chains of glucose molecules. These chains can contain as few as 4 and as many as 400 sugar molecules. (Shorter-chain starches are water-soluble; longer-chain starches are not water soluble.) The glucose chains are connected by ether linkages. An ether linkage happens when two sugar molecules join together and one water molecule is removed. During the process of mashing, enzymes cause water molecules to be reintroduced to the ether linkages, breaking the link, thus freeing the sugars from the chain.

There are two main stages in the process of converting starches to fermentable sugars: liquefaction and saccharification. During liquefaction, the alpha-amylase enzymes convert long-chain insoluble starches to water-soluble short-chain starches. Next, beta-amylase enzymes reduce short-chain starches to sugar molecules (saccharification).

Malted grains (usually barley) supply the enzymes needed for starch conversion.

Mash temperatures must be maintained precisely in order to get the maximum levels of fermentable sugars out of the grain without damaging the critical enzymes. The optimum temperature range for alpha-amylase is 67°–71°C/152°–160°F; for beta-amylase, it is 60°–66°C/140°–151°F.

What About Gluten?

A lot of people these days are going gluten-free, whether because of allergies or personal choice. Wheat and rye and barley are all "gluten" grains; corn and rice are not. Many people are understandably confused when it comes to things like beer and whiskey; since they are made from ingredients known to contain gluten, they cannot legally be labeled "gluten-free." The fact is, though, that distilled liquor, no matter what it is made from, does *not* contain gluten.

I'm sure some people with severe gluten allergies or celiac disease are simply avoiding grain-based beverages, just to eliminate the possibility of a bad reaction. Celiac.com states unequivocally that distilled spirits do not contain gluten; however, that site has many comments from people who say they have had a reaction to this liquor or that, blaming the reaction on gluten. The good news is, since you're now learning just what happens during the mashing process, the facts about gluten and distilled liquor will make sense to you. A basic understanding of what gluten is will also help.

Gluten is a gummy, stretchy *protein*. It is formed when the precursor proteins glutenin and gliadin link. Good bread flour is higher in protein than pastry or all-purpose flour. That's because the higher the protein, the more gluten develops during fermentation, giving the bread dough its structure and elasticity.

When grains are mashed, their starches are converted to *sugars*. Those sugars are then in suspension in the

Since the temperature range that favors alpha-amylase results in a mash that is high in non-fermentable sugars, it's best to hold the temperature in the range that favors beta-amylase. The alpha-amylase will still work; its action is just slowed down by the cooler temperature. If a constant temperature can be maintained for 60 to 90 minutes, then 63°C/145°F is the optimum conversion temperature. Otherwise, it's better to aim for a conversion temperature of 66°C/150°F. The temperature will slowly drop to about 60°C/140°F during the rest, so the temperature actually stays within the ideal range for conversion.

mashing liquid and are drained off to be fermented and distilled. What's left of the grain? It usually still has a small amount of carbohydrate, since the mashing process rarely is 100 percent efficient. For the most part, though, what's left in the grain is protein, fiber and trace minerals (see sidebar below about feeding mashed grains to livestock).

You see the point? Carbohydrates are removed from the grain; protein (and therefore gluten) is left behind. Even if some of the gluten were to survive all the previous processes and make it into your still, it would stay in the boiling pot because it simply would not travel through the still as a vapor.

There are many possible reasons for people to have reactions to alcoholic drinks. Sulfites in wine cause reactions in some; in others, for example diabetics, the sugar content of alcohol can cause problems. You probably know at least one person who can't drink any alcohol at all without becoming hopelessly inebriated. There are also additives in many distilled spirit products, such as coloring and flavoring, which many people are sensitive to.

If you have a reaction of some kind when you drink alcohol, don't be so quick to blame it on gluten. If you know you can't easily tolerate a certain beverage, of course it is a good idea to avoid it. But if you're gluten-free, I hope you are convinced that there is no reason to avoid making and enjoying your own grain-based distilled spirits.

All these enzymes are quickly inactivated by temperatures above 71°C/160°F, and can result in incomplete starch conversion. Temperatures of 76°C/168°F or above will instantly denature the enzymes. So if you are adding amylase enzymes to the mash, do not add them at mash temperatures; instead, add them to the fermentation bucket when the mash temperature is right for pitching the yeast.

Water

A topic of much debate among distillers is what kind of water is best. Mashing water should be as nearly devoid of iron as possible. High iron content will destroy the enzymes needed for starch conversion. A fairly high calcium content, however, is beneficial to the fermentation process and contributes to the ultimate flavor of the spirit.

If the water is low in calcium and you want to add calcium, use calcium sulphate (gypsum) rather than calcium carbonate (precipitated chalk).

If you want to have your water tested, the important things to find out are: overall hardness level (ideally hardness level 8 or less), iron content (ideally less than 25 parts per million [ppm]), calcium content and pH.

If you are using distilled or deionized water, adding 2 teaspoons (10 ml) gypsum per 20 liters water will bring the calcium level to about 150 ppm. We are fortunate that our spring-fed water supply is naturally high in calcium and completely free of iron.

pH of the Mash Water

Optimum pH of mash water is 5.2 to 5.5. I find that adding 2½ cups (625 ml) backset to 5 gallons (19 L) of mash water is just right with our spring water, which has a pH of exactly 7.0 (neutral). Alternatively, for instance if I have no backset on hand, I add 2 teaspoons (10 ml) citric acid. Tartaric acid may also be used. Some books suggest using 95% sulphuric acid to increase acidity, but it can be dangerous to handle. If you make wine at home, you probably already have some citric acid and/or tartaric acid, so use those to acidify your water.

 TIP *The conversion process itself tends to lower the pH of the mash somewhat, so aim for your mash water to be about pH 5.8 to 6.0 before adding the grains.*

It's unusual to need to adjust the water pH upward, that is, in the case of the water being too acidic. Calcium carbonate (precipitated chalk) may be used to make this adjustment when necessary.

Common Grains
Used for Small-scale Distilling

Barley

In the last 50 years, the yields from barley have increased by around 30 percent. Today, about 25 percent of the barley grown worldwide is used for brewing and distilling.

Six-row malt generally has the highest *diastatic power*, that is, the ability to efficiently convert starches to sugars (see sidebar What Is Malt?). Because six-row barley kernels are smaller than those of two-row barley, six-row barley has more kernels per kilo; more kernels means more enzymes. These days, though, modified two-row pale malt is nearly as high in diastatic power as the six-row type.

Pale ale and light lager malts have high diastatic power; they are also usually less expensive than other malt choices. Caramelized and roasted malts retain little of their diastatic power. I have had good consistent results using two-row pale ale malt for just about everything.

By today's standards, you need roughly 2.2 pounds (1 kg) of malted barley to make one 25-ounce (750-ml) bottle of whiskey at 40% ABV.

Wheat

The alcohol industry uses winter wheat almost exclusively. With a higher starch content, it can produce more alcohol per bushel of grain. Spring wheat is higher in protein so it is better for baking bread. Wheat malt has high diastatic power.

Corn

American commercial distillers use dent corn for making whiskey. Corn gives higher alcohol yield than other cereals due to its higher sugar and starch content; in fact, dent corn typically is 85 percent starch, compared to roughly 50 percent for barley.

Rye

Always add some rye to bourbon; it contributes a pepperiness and dryness that balance out the sweetness of the corn. Rye can also be

What Is Malt?

Any kind of grain can be malted, although barley is the most commonly used malted grain in producing liquor. Malting is a process in which grains are moistened and allowed to sprout. When sprouting begins, the grain produces enzymes that break down the starchy endosperm to provide nourishment for the growing plant. In the malting process, the grain is heated in a kiln shortly after it has sprouted; this stops the growing process and preserves the endosperm and enzymes that would be consumed if the grain continued to grow. These enzymes are critical in the conversion of starch to fermentable sugar during mashing. The diastatic enzymes produced during malting are the ones that convert starch to sugar, so when you buy malted grains, look for those with high diastatic power.

grown in colder climates than other cereal grains. It is a winter crop, sown in the fall and harvested early the following summer.

Rye has particularly high levels of a starch group called beta-glucan, which is very sticky and gummy. Rye malt also has high diastatic power.

Milling

Milling barley increases the surface area of the grain and separates the husk from the interior of the grain, allowing better starch-to-sugar conversion rates. Milling malted barley also effectively turns the husks into a natural filtering system that keeps tiny particles from draining out of the wash. When milling malted barley, it is preferable to split the husks rather than crushing them to powder; this creates a better medium for efficient percolation.

Particle size is of critical importance during mashing and fermentation, and can have a noticeable effect on alcohol yield. For example, in malt whiskey production, the barley is milled to a flaky powder called grist.

Malting Your Own Grains

I have had some fun experimenting with malting my own grain. At first my main reason for doing this was that, at least in our area, it's difficult to find organic malt. (I know I can order it, but I'd be spending a fortune on shipping for the quantities I wanted.) I was able to buy organic barley from our friend Nash Huber, a well-known local farmer.

I learned the basics of malting from the excellent description of the process in Ian Smiley's book *Making Pure Corn Whiskey* (see Books in Appendix A). This year I plan to build a solar-powered food dryer and adapt it for drying the malt. My feeling is that learning about malting has helped me to better understand the mashing process, and it's a fascinating process itself. However, in most areas, high-quality malt is easy to find and fairly inexpensive, so I would recommend using commercial malt at least while you are starting out with mashing.

Why Go to All This Trouble to Extract the Sugar?
Why Not Just Use Sugar?

Proponents of making "sugar-shine" (see chapter 13) like to make this argument. Since the object of mashing is to extract fermentable sugar, the argument goes, isn't it more efficient to just start with sugar? Hmm. Possibly, I grant you, it may save you a little time. All you have to do is dissolve sugar in water, add yeast and ferment it, right? OK, right. My response is that if efficiency was all that mattered, commercial distilleries would make their liquor that way. Instead, after all these years and with all the scientific advances, they still mash grains to make whiskey or vodka or gin. (I also grant you that making rum is essentially dissolving molasses or sugar in water, fermenting and distilling it. But let's keep the subject to grain-based liquor for the moment.)

First, in almost all cases, making alcohol from grains is much cheaper than making it from pure sugar. And second, generations of savvy distillers have known that, for many complicated reasons, grain that is mashed yields liquor with a lot more character and flavor. Corn mash gives you bourbon, but adding more or less rye to the mash can result in more complex flavor profiles. Since part of my object in writing *Craft Distilling* is to encourage you to make

The Iodine Starch Test

How can you tell if your mash has completed its starch conversion? An easy method is the iodine starch test. Collect a few drops of the clear liquid at the top of your mash. Dab the liquid onto a clean white porcelain saucer or plate. Add a drop or two of tincture of iodine into the sample. If any starch is present, the liquid will instantly turn blue. The color won't change noticeably if all the starch has been converted to sugar.

Note: Discard the sample after testing; do not return the sample to your mash.

high-quality spirits, I hope you will keep an open mind, read on and give me a chance to convince you it is worth it.

Non-malt Cereals

Non-malt cereals (i.e., unmalted corn, wheat or rye) must be cooked first (before adding malt to the mash) to gelatinize the starches. For example, corn is boiled at 100°C/212°F; this causes the starches to swell irreversibly and breaks the hydrogen bonds. Later, when the mash is cooler and the milled malt is added, the enzymes in the malt can easily begin converting the gelatinized starches.

Rye is cooked at 78°C/172°F; wheat, like malt, is mashed at about 65°C/149°F.

Mashed grains (left) after being strained from the wash (right). Mashed grains are fed out to our poultry.

Using Glucoamylase in the Mashing Process

Dextrins and polysaccharides (non-fermentable sugars) are produced during the mash process when malt enzymes are used. Glucoamylase converts these to fermentable sugars.

A good substitute for glucoamylase is *Beano*: 5 drops of the liquid type or 3 tablets (crushed) is adequate for about 6.5 gallons (25 L) of mash.

Rhysozyme (also known as koji) is an enzyme used to make the rice wine called sake. It is one of the best forms of glucoamylase you can use for making whiskey. Many homebrew shops carry rhysozyme (see Ingredients in Appendix A).

Tip: ½ teaspoon (2 ml) amylase per gallon of mash will increase yields by 10 to 20 percent. Add it after the hydration period (the first hour) when mashing.

What to Do with the Grains Once Mashing Is Complete

You may well be wondering what happens to all those beautiful grains once they have been milled and mashed. Remembering that the mashing process has removed the majority of the starches in the grain, what is left? Largely protein and fiber. These grains make an excellent feed for all kinds of livestock. For example, if you are making bourbon, your mash is probably between 50 percent and 80 percent corn. This is a terrific feed for pigs, who (I speak from experience) will be thrilled. If you have an all-malt mash, you might want to mix it with your usual feed so as to provide more balanced nutrition. I have also heard of people using the mashed grains to make bread or other baked goods. Certainly you can compost it if you like, but if you have poultry or other livestock (or your neighbor does), I think it's a great option to use mashed grains as a feed supplement.

I wish I could take credit for it, but actually this is not a new idea. Large commercial distilleries in the Midwest have been doing it for years. Usually the grains are dried before being passed on to local farmers; this makes it easier to store the grains before use without the risk of mold or other spoilage. I recently heard about a small craft brewery in our area that was actively looking for people to take their mashed grains. It's such a great idea because it works on a small scale as well as on the large scale. Here it's usually a bucket at a time, and it's almost always fed out to our chickens, turkeys and ducks the same day.

Remember: Never dump mashed grains into sewer systems! It places too much pressure on the system and may cause blockages. (Yes, I have heard of this happening.)

Guidelines for Feeding Mashed Grains to Livestock

Feed out the grain while it is fresh and warm. Check the pH of the mash first; if it is below 4.0, add feed-lime to raise it to between 5 and 6. (This shouldn't be necessary if it is fed out promptly.)

Recommended maximum amounts to be fed each day:

- Cattle: 8 to 10 gallons (30 to 40 L)
- Sheep and hogs: 0.5 to 0.7 gallons (2 to 3 L)
- Horses: 2.6 to 3.9 gallons (10 to 15 L)

Mill Your Own or Buy It Milled?

Most homebrew supply shops will gladly mill your grains for you, usually for a minimal additional cost. However, if you want to buy your malt or other grains by the bag (often a much more economical choice), you will almost always have to mill it yourself. Last year, I finally decided to buy a grain mill specifically designed for milling grains to be mashed. Previously I had been using an old Corona hand-crank grain mill that my husband has had for years. Not only was it extremely tiring (unless I was only grinding a very small amount), the milling consistency varied. Some of it was ground virtually to flour; other grains came through nearly intact. Not too surprising that I was getting mixed results with my mashing using those grains!

I'm quite happy with the new grain mill, although I definitely want to build some kind of stand for it; it's designed to sit on top of a 5- or 6-gallon bucket. I've found it's easiest to use when I'm sitting down with the bucket in front of me. But the bucket is so lightweight that it moves around a lot, and it's tiring using one hand to constantly hold everything down while cranking with the other hand. Plus I'm leaning forward during all this in a way that I'm quite sure is far from ergonomically correct. (What can I say, I'm not getting any younger.) It has occurred to me that if I take the handle part off the crank, it looks like I could chuck the crankshaft into an electric drill, but somehow that never seems to occur to me when I'm actually using the damn thing.

My hand-crank grain mill, the perfect tool for crushing grains before mashing.

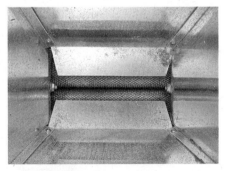

The heavy rollers of my grain mill. The gap between is adjustable.

Using DME or Liquid Malt Extract

If you make your own beer, chances are you've used either DME (dried malt extract) or liquid malt extract at some point. You might be wondering about using these extracts for making whiskey. Of course, it would be quicker and easier than milling a lot of grain and mashing it yourself, since the mashing has been done for you. However, these are relatively expensive alternatives, just one of the reasons why commercial distilleries don't use them. I'm all in favor of making really high-quality liquor, and this usually means using methods that take a bit longer but eventually pay off. If you're serious about learning to be a good distiller, take the time to learn to mash your own grains. After a lot of practice, I'm still improving the efficiency of my mashing technique, resulting in improved yields and flavor quality.

Tip: Do not attempt to use DME or liquid malt extract in place of malted barley when mashing. Because of the heat involved in the process of making malt extracts, they no longer contain any diastatic enzymes and will be useless for starch conversion.

Fermentation

Fermentation is the biochemical process that converts sugar to alcohol and carbon dioxide, through the action of yeast enzymes called zymase. Yeast metabolizes both aerobically (in the presence of oxygen) and anaerobically (in the absence of oxygen).

In the early stages of fermentation, when yeast is added to the sugary wort, it is rapidly multiplying by using sugar to form new cell material (aerobic stage). After all the dissolved oxygen in the mash has been consumed, the yeast stops multiplying and enters the anaerobic stage, converting the sugar in the mash to alcohol and carbon dioxide.

Yeast needs nutrients such as amino acids and nitrogen to be healthy and multiply rapidly. If you attempt to ferment plain sugar dissolved in water, you will need to add large amounts of yeast to compensate for the lack of nutrients in the wash. The yeast simply won't need to multiply as much if there are already sufficient yeast cells present to ferment the available sugars. However, under these conditions, with no added yeast nutrients, you will rarely end up with a wash of more than about 8% ABV before the yeast dies off and stops fermenting.

Aeration of the Wash

Grain mash is loaded with both nutrients and fermentable sugars. It does benefit from the addition of dissolved oxygen during the early aerobic phase of fermentation, though. For small batches, simply pouring the mash back and forth vigorously between two clean fermentation buckets 4 to 6 times will adequately oxygenate the mash.

It is not recommended to use bottled oxygen to aerate your wash. Excess oxygen will interfere with desirable ester production, which is especially important when making whiskey.

Unlike the process of making beer or wine, where the mash typically undergoes both a primary and secondary fermentation, a mash to be distilled goes through only primary fermentation. In fact, grain mashes usually ferment no more than 72 to 80 hours before they are distilled. A secondary fermentation would actually adversely affect the ester profile of the mash, resulting in unpleasant-tasting liquor.

Once the fermentable sugars have been used up, the yeast metabolism changes and begins breaking down and consuming nonfermentable sugars and other organic compounds. This process involves enzymes like permease that lead to the formation of undesirable flavors. This can be avoided, however, by using glucoamylase enzymes to ensure a minimum of non-fermentable sugars.

As fermentation progresses, the wash acidifies, eventually lowering the pH to about 3.5. This helps control the growth of unwanted bacteria, which can't survive this kind of acidic environment. If your recipe calls for added bacteria such as lactobacillus, add it to the wash when you add the yeast.

Try this: Add lactobacillus bacteria first, then wait to add the yeast. The bacteria will lower the pH of the wash. This will prevent the yeast from forming some of the acids it normally makes, which in turn will noticeably affect the acid and ester profile of the whiskey. I suggest checking the pH of the wash frequently before pitching your yeast, though, and don't wait too long to add the yeast. Start with a delay of 4 to 6 hours after adding the bacteria and experiment from there.

Generally the wash should be distilled as soon as vigorous fermentation stops or slows down to occasional bubbling. Plan to begin distillation once the specific gravity of the wash has dropped to 1.015 or below.

It's important to distill the wash promptly once fermentation has slowed down or stopped. Once active fermentation has slowed considerably, the mash can be vulnerable to invasion by spoilage bacteria if left too long before distilling. In addition, the alcohol produced during fermentation can be lost through oxidation. I highly recommend that you check your schedule before starting to ferment a wash destined to be distilled, to make sure you will have the time to distill the wash promptly.

Specific Gravity

Specific gravity (SG) is a measure of the density of a liquid relative to water. By definition, the specific gravity of water is 1.000. If a liquid were exactly twice as dense as water, its SG would be 2.000.

SG is used to measure the amount of sugar dissolved in the wash. Dissolved sugar increases the density of the mash; a solution of 1% sugar has a specific gravity of 1.004, a 2% solution's SG is 1.008 and so on. SG is useful for determining when fermentation is slowing down or done; the SG may drop below 1.000, because the presence of alcohol and the absence of sugar make the wash less dense than water.

I encourage you to get in the habit of checking and recording the SG of each batch of wash prior to fermentation (see Appendix C for a sample record-keeping form). A typical grain mash will have an originating gravity (OG) of 1.060 to 1.070. This is an ideal range to aim for. An OG below 1.060 will work, but the yield of alcohol will naturally be lower. A mash with an OG of over 1.070 will produce upwards of 10% alcohol or more; at that point, the yeast metabolism changes slightly and may affect the flavor profile of the liquor produced. However, you should not encounter this issue if you use a yeast strain developed specifically for distilling.

My hydrometer is a common triple-scale model, easily found at homebrew supply shops. It shows the specific gravity, as well as the sugar content as a Brix number, and the potential alcohol of the liquid based on the amount of sugar available. Brix is another method of expressing the amount of sugar in a liquid; a reading of Brix 16, for example, means the sample contains 16% sugar.

To measure the SG of your mash using a hydrometer, make sure your test cylinder and hydrometer are clean, and place the cylinder on a level surface. Pour a sample of the wash, as nearly free of solids as possible, into the test cylinder; about three-quarters full is about right. Gently place the hydrometer into the liquid in the cylinder and let it come to rest, floating in the liquid. Look at the scale on the stem of the hydrometer, reading the number where the liquid contacts the hydrometer in the center of the cylinder.

Most hydrometers of this type are calibrated at 15.56°C/60°F. If the sample tested is not at this temperature, you will need to adjust the reading. Hydrometers come with a conversion scale to make this easy.

You can also use a Brix or sugar refractometer to measure the sugar content of your wash. If you make wine from fresh grapes or other fruit, you may already have one of these handy tools. The advantage of a refractometer is that it uses only a few drops of a liquid to measure the sugar; grape growers often use one to assess the ripeness of grapes before harvest, based on the their sugar content. The main disadvantage is that it is a much more expensive option than a hydrometer and test cylinder, but you may find it better fits your style of doing things.

Types of Yeast

Distilling yeasts tend to be very attenuative, i.e., they result in a wash of low specific gravity at the end of fermentation. Try experimenting with different strains of beer yeasts. When using beer yeast, be sure to make a starter of at least one-half gallon (2 L), using sterilized wort, to ensure a desirable pitching rate (see sidebar on Yeast Starters).

The type of yeast affects the yield of alcohol, can influence the rate and intensity of the fermentation process and contributes to the complex flavor profile ultimately created.

Malt whiskey requires about 44 pounds (20 kg) of dry yeast for each ton of barley fermented. This works out to about ⅙ ounce

Turbo Yeasts and Others to Avoid

The popular "Turbo" yeasts are typically formulated to ferment 11 to 17.6 pounds (5 to 8 kg) sugar dissolved in 6.6 gallons (25 L) of water. This generally results in a wash of 13% to 20% alcohol. You'd think that this would speed up the distillation process by starting out with a relatively high alcohol level, right? It can take up to 2 weeks to ferment out a sugar wash to near 20% alcohol. Turbo yeast is a high-alcohol-tolerance yeast with yeast nutrients added to it. It can be good for making gin or vodka, if you want to make those from sugar and water. However, it really doesn't do much for grain-mash fermentations, as it was designed to ferment nutrient-poor washes like sugar water. Also, high-alcohol-tolerant yeasts like Turbo yeast and champagne yeast are not suitable for producing desirable flavors in whiskies.

(5 g) per liter of wort. Some hobby distillers advocate using huge amounts of yeast, suggesting that it doesn't hurt, and may result in increased alcohol production. While I do recommend experimenting with yeast quantity to some extent (always remembering to keep records!), overdoing the yeast is wasteful at best, and may adversely affect the flavor of some spirits, especially whiskey.

I don't recommend using baker's yeast for distilling; it produces undesirable flavors.

Gert Strand of Malmo, Sweden, produces the Prestige brand distilling yeast. This yeast, available in small quantities for hobby distillers, produces excellent flavor and yields. (It can be bought online at whiskeyyeast.com but is often more economical through homebrew supply shops. See Ingredients in Appendix A.)

Yeast Starters

If your wash has an OG of 1.070 or more, I recommend using a yeast starter. Those poor little yeast cells can be overwhelmed in the presence of such an abundance of sugars, and may die out before all the sugar has been converted to alcohol. The idea of a starter is to increase the number of yeast cells before adding the yeast to the fermenter, to jump-start the fermentation process.

To make a yeast starter for 5 gallons (19 L) of wash, set aside 1 to 2 pints (500 to 1,000 ml) of fresh wort at room temperature. Use a glass or translucent plastic container. Pitch your yeast into the wort, shake well and let sit for 1 or 2 days. After a day or so, you should begin to see layers of yeast sediment at the bottom of the container. You can now add the starter to the wash in the fermenter.

You can also try making a yeast starter to "proof" yeast that is past its use-by date. Some yeast cells will still be viable up to about a year, so it is worth trying. However, it's best to always use fresh yeast, so try not to buy more than you need at one time.

Pitching the Yeast

Why this is called "pitching" I have no idea. Moving on! Put the fermenter in a place where it can be left undisturbed for at least 3 days. Ideally the ambient temperature should be 21°–33°C/70°–90°F. It's important to keep the temperature of the mash below 38°C/100°F. Add the yeast and enzymes (if using). After about 30 minutes the yeast will be hydrated and can be stirred into the mash.

For 5 gallons (19 L) wash:
- ⅓ cup (75 ml) distiller's yeast plus 1 teaspoon (5 ml) distillery glucoamylase OR
- 1 package yeast/enzyme combination

Fermentations with Grains in the Mash

If you are making bourbon or another kind of whiskey that calls for leaving the grains in the mash during fermentation, you will need to strain the grains out before transferring the wash to your still (unless your still is enormous; see sidebar below). After straining, the volume of liquid should be about 70 percent of the total volume of the mash. Let the liquid settle for 30 to 60 minutes, then check the terminating gravity (TG).

The percentage of alcohol in the wash can be calculated using the following formula:

$$\frac{1000\,(OG-TG)}{7.4} = \%\,ABV$$

For example: Say you have a bourbon wash to distill. The OG was 1.062, the TG 1.008. Using this formula, subtract 1.008 from 1.062 and get 0.054. Multiply that by 1,000 to get 54; 54 divided by 7.4 is 7.29. So the estimated alcohol content of your fermented wash is 7.29%. Don't forget to record this number! You can use it to calcu-

Fermenting With and Without the Grains

In all my reading about whiskey production, I have yet to discover why some kinds of whiskey are fermented with the grains left in, while others have the grains strained out and the liquid alone is fermented. Some types, notably bourbon, are also distilled with the grains left in. In the process of making Irish whiskey, the liquid is drained from the grains before fermentation. Why is this, anyway?

I keep hoping someone will give me the answer to this burning question. I hope it's not going to turn out that it's just tradition or something. Actually, I suspect that, during fermentation, the yeast might scavenge additional sugars and amino acids from the grains, making it beneficial to leave the grains in there. As fermentation progresses and the wort becomes more acidic and alcoholic, though, it seems to me that undesirable flavor elements might start creeping in. This might explain why distillers are taught to distill

promptly once fermentation has slowed way down.

I don't distill anything with the grains left in, for the simple reason that my still's boiling pot is too small. When I mash grains for a typical 5-gallon batch of whiskey, I use around 15 pounds of grains and 6 gallons of water. I have to use my 10-gallon restaurant-grade stainless steel stockpot for this, and believe me, that pot is at least three-quarters full once all the grains are in there. My still's boiling pot holds a maximum of about 7½ gallons, so there you go.

Why don't I just make smaller batches at a time? First of all, that's not efficient. I like to put as much as I can in the still without risking boilovers; in my case, the most I distill at once is 15 liters. Second, the bottom of my boiling pot isn't very thick, and no doubt I would risk burning grains near the bottom while the still was heating up.

late the total amount of ethanol in your still, which in turn will help you estimate how much to expect in the heads, hearts and tails runs later on.

Before distilling, let strained wash settle for 12 to 24 hours. Siphon the liquid into the still, leaving behind as much sediment as possible.

Typical fermentation times for whiskey:

• Malt whiskey, 50 to 100 hours
• Irish whiskey, 60 to 120 hours
• Bourbon and rye whiskey, 3 to 5 days (fermented with the grains in the fermentation bucket).

Fermentation usually slows after about 36 hours; most distilleries stop the fermentation after 48 to 60 hours, depending on what is being made.

Certain spoilage bacteria can produce methanol. If your mash develops a rotten or "off" smell during fermentation, throw it away! Do not distill and drink it.

Bacterial Fermentation

Although bacterial fermentation is rarely mentioned among hobby distillers, I think it is worth a brief discussion. As you gain some experience with fermentation and distilling, you may want to experiment with it yourself.

Esters are compounds that are formed when an alcohol molecule bonds chemically with an acid molecule. This bonding process happens during all stages of liquor production. Different yeast strains produce different ester profiles during fermentation (just as in beer production), and free acids in solution eventually form additional esters during the aging process of spirits such as whiskey and brandy.

Free acids are found in oak barrels, as well as in the various yeasts and bacteria naturally present in the wash. Some lactobacillus bacteria, for example, produce lactic acid, while other strains produce other kinds of volatile acids when they consume sugar during fermentation. (Those of you who make cheese will be familiar with this acidification process.) When these acids bond with alcohol, they "esterify" into a wide variety of flavors such as fruity and floral notes. For example, lactic acid esterifies with ethanol into ethyl lactate, which tastes like butter cream. Lactobacillus can even consume other acids, changing them into different ones, resulting in unique flavors.

Lactobacillus is most active at the beginning and end of fermentation. It is more or less dormant during the anaerobic phase, when yeast is most active. This bacteria, especially *L. thermophilus* ("heat-loving"), which is already present in the air and on the grain you use, survives the heat of fermentation during sugar conversion and continues to multiply. Its reproduction slows down as the pH of the wash drops during fermentation, but it becomes more active as the yeast cells start to die off. At this point, the lactobacillus consumes nutrients in the yeast sediment and any residual sugar it finds. As it eats, it begins to produce the acids that will later form esters.

There are many different strains of lactobacillus. For the hobby distiller, it is convenient to find them in small freeze-dried packets where cheese- and yogurt-making supplies are sold. Homebrew shops often also carry a refrigerated liquid form. You can add the bacteria to your wash when you pitch the yeast; or, try adding it several hours *before* adding the yeast. They will produce different acids (and therefore different esters) depending on which phase of fermentation they are most active.

Products of Fermentation

- Ethyl alcohol: Lighter than water (1 gallon ethanol = 6.6 lb; 1 gallon water = 8.3 lb).

- Glycerin: An oily, sweet-tasting liquid. Important element in wine-making, as it makes wine more full-bodied. One liter of wine has about ¼ to ⅔ oz. (6 to 9 g) glycerin. Glycerin does not transfer during distillation.
- CO_2: Heavier than air.
- Acetaldehyde: Natural by-product of distillation. Production increases sharply when fermentation is poor. Boils at about 20°C/68°F, so it can easily be removed when wash is properly heated. Pungent odor and taste that are undesirable in distillates.
- Fusel oils (fusel alcohols): Higher-order alcohols with boiling points of 80°–160°C/176°–320°F. Unpleasant smell and taste. If ABV of low wines in a spirit run is less than 42%, fusel oils are more rapidly transferred to the distillate.

Overview of the Distilling Process and Techniques

By now you're no doubt itching to get on to the next part of the process, the actual distilling of your spirit. You've mashed your grains, fermented the wash...now what?

I can't stress too much the importance of taking your time, especially if you are new to distilling. It took at least half a dozen distilling runs before I was even starting to get comfortable with the process. Up till then, I spent all my spare minutes in the stillhouse rereading the instructions umpteen times, kind of like when I was first learning to use my pressure canner. But I digress.

Some home distilling books tell you to do all your distilling in one go. Theoretically, using a column still (and assuming you have some experience), it is possible to distill a good-quality spirit in one distilling run. For now, though, I think it's a better idea to plan two distilling runs; I'll tell you why in a minute. Some spirits require a third distillation run (Irish whiskey), and vodka is sometimes distilled four times or even more. While you're learning, let's focus on a basic two-run distilling process.

First Distillation: The Beer-stripping Run

Technically, a fractionating still such as mine is capable of distilling whiskey in a single distillation run. However, when distilling most liquors, I prefer the two-run process, which involves a relatively fast "beer-stripping" run, followed by a spirit run.

The beer-stripping run is straightforward. No separation of heads, hearts and tails happens during this run; the intent is merely to concentrate the alcohol in the wash. Some impurities are also separated during this process. The resulting distillate is called low wines. The low wines, depending on the ABV of the wash, typically will come out at 20% to 25% ABV. For example, if the ABV of your wash is between 5% and 10%, you can expect to collect low wines of between 21% and 27% ABV.

Theoretically, up to one third of the wash will be collected as low wines in a stripping run. Depending on what I am distilling, I generally get between 2 and 3 liters of low wines from 15 liters of wash at about 10% ABV. Naturally, the amount of low wines you collect will vary depending on the ABV of your wash.

After all the work you've done to this point, mashing and fermenting your wash, don't risk ruining it now by being in a hurry. It's best to heat the still slowly to avoid burning the wash. My boiling pot doesn't have a very thick bottom, so I've learned to be careful about this. With a little experience, you'll know how high to set the heat so it heats the wash efficiently but without burning. I used a Sharpie pen to mark the regulator dial on my propane burner; anything I can do to ensure a consistent process seems like a good idea to me. Once again: Keep notes!

Procedure

Plan ahead before a distilling session. It's important not to be distracted or need to step away from the still once you've begun heating it. Over the first few batches I ran through my still, I found that it consistently takes between 2 and 2¼ hours for a beer-stripping run to finish once I start heating the still. Most of the time you will not be actively involved, especially in the early part when you are wait-ing for the low wines to emerge. It can't be over-emphasized: **Never leave the still unattended once it is heating.**

So bring something with you to read, or your iPod or unpaid bills or whatever. I often get a lot of writing done in the couple of hours I am in my stillhouse! It's about a hundred yards from our house, so I'm not distracted by the phone or tempted to go bake cookies or change the oil in the truck or something.

Don't forget to limit the amount of wash in the still to no more than three-quarters full to minimize the risk of boilovers. My boil-ing pot has a 25-liter capacity, but I never load more than 15 liters into it. (I've only had it come close to boiling over one time, and that was when I had loaded it with 19 liters of wash.) Also, when trans-ferring the wash to the still, try to minimize the amount of sediment that ends up in the still. It may burn when the wash is heated, and will adversely affect the flavor of the spirit.

Finally, a use for flour-and-water paste. Once you've assembled your still, it's a good idea to seal the seams and any potential leaks before turning up the heat. A simple flour-and-water paste works great for this. Mix some all-purpose flour with enough cool water to make a thick paste, and spread it around the joints on your still. The paste will harden and form a tight seal as the still heats up. If there happens to be an unexpected buildup of pressure in the still (usually due to a clog somewhere in the system), the paste will give way at the joints, preventing a possible explosion.

You'll just have to get used to me reminding you to make notes. Keeping records of your distilling runs will simplify things for you as you gain experience. For example, I learned early on that my still, with 15 liters of wash, consistently comes to a boil in 60 minutes. (However, my stillhouse is unheated, and this figure is based on the assumption that my wash was fermenting in the house and brought out and loaded into the still roughly at room temperature.) I also marked the regulator on the propane burner so I can be sure I set the flame at the same level every time.

On my still, although I can easily vary the flow rate of the distillate using the needle valve, for beer-stripping runs, I leave the valve wide open. Once the low wines start to drip, I do slow the flow rate a bit, though; this minimizes the amount of alcohol left in the still by ensuring some degree of reflux and separation. However, in general, I prefer to vary the flow rate by turning down the heat just a bit. Although this naturally slows the process down, it has the advantage of preventing the condenser water from heating up, so it actually increases efficiency.

Beware of slowing the rate too much, though; if you're making

Important Safety Notes about the Condenser

The still's condenser should be a minimum of four feet from the still's heat source, especially if the still is heated with an open flame.

It's important to start running cooling water through the condenser well before the first distillate begins to flow. It's a good idea to get in the habit of monitoring the temperature of the wash as it heats. I have a thermometer that measures the temperature of the wash in the boiling pot, and I usually turn the condenser water on when the wash is about 60°C/140°F. This generally is about 30 minutes after I start heating the wash.

Don't let it get much hotter than this before you begin to run the cold water; the alcohol will begin vaporizing well before its boiling point of 78.3°C/173°F, so you may lose some ethanol this way if the condenser is not working yet.

If the cooling water in the condenser is allowed to overheat, it will pass through the condenser into the air as alcohol steam. This steam is both flammable and explosive! Never leave the still unattended, and don't ever succumb to the temptation to try to speed up the process by turning up the heat.

whiskey or other flavor-positive spirits, slowing the flow rate will tend to strip out too many of the desirable congeners that are critical to the final flavor of the spirit. So take your time; for small batches like these, the difference in time is minimal, and I promise the results will be worth it.

The still head temperature will be about 80°C/176°F when the low wines start to drip. The temperature will rise to 98°C/208°F as the ethanol in the still is depleted. I usually end the stripping run once the still head temperature has reached 98°C/208°F. Typically the emerging distillate will be around 10% ABV at this point, and I don't think it's worth the extra fuel and time needed to recover just a little more ethanol.

Calculating Ethanol in the Low Wines

Once you've finished the stripping run, it's a good idea to calculate how much ethanol at 100% ABV is in your low wines. This will help you estimate quantities of heads, hearts and tails in the spirit run. Of course, your actual yield will depend on how accurately you make the cuts between heads, hearts and tails, but the number will still be a useful guide. Here is the formula:

Volume of low wines ×
ABV of low wines =
Volume of 100% ethanol in the still

For example, say I have 2,190 ml of low wines at 40% ABV.

2,190 × 0.40 = 876 ml of ethanol at 100% ABV

Advanced tip: If you are adding feints (explained below) to the low wines in your spirit run, the calculation formula is as follows:

(Vol of low wines × ABV of low wines) +
(Vol of feints × ABV of feints) =
Vol of 100% ethanol in still

Tip: Appendix C has a simple form you can use to record all these numbers, as well as the actual volumes of heads, hearts and tails collected during your distillation runs.

The stripping run also, in my opinion, makes it easier to judge and make the cuts in the subsequent spirit run. With small batches like these, the cuts can happen very quickly; for a relatively inexperienced distiller like myself, every possible advantage is worth pursuing. What I like to do is ferment two large batches of the same type at once. I then do stripping runs; usually this means 3 or 4 batches in my still. I then have a good amount of low wines to work with. This is a more efficient use of the still. Also the more volume of low

Low wines, feints and hearts. Masking tape and a Sharpie pen are handy for labeling.

wines, the longer the transition times between the heads, hearts and tails, making it that much easier to accurately judge and make the cuts.

When your stripping run is finished, be sure to record the amount of low wines collected and the aggregate ABV of the low wines. The low wines can now be redistilled in a spirit run, or saved to add to low wines from additional stripping runs. I like to store low wines in clean 1-gallon glass bottles retrieved from local businesses. Half-gallon Mason jars also work well. Remember to clearly mark each jar or bottle; low wines all look alike! I use blue masking tape and a Sharpie pen for this.

Second Distillation: The Spirit Run

Once the wash is concentrated into low wines of around 25% ABV, it is much easier to monitor the ABV of the distillate and the still head temperature, and to make the cuts at the right time. As previously noted, the more volume of low wines in your spirit run, the longer the transitions between the cuts.

Important note: It is even more critical to avoid over-filling the still for a spirit run. Ethanol expands when heated, and the low wines you will use in your spirit run have a much higher concentration of ethanol than the wash used in your stripping run. I am probably over-cautious, but I usually don't fill my boiling pot more than half-full for spirit runs, depending on the ABV of the low wines.

Assuming your still has a quality thermometer that is accurately placed, still head temperature monitoring is fairly straightforward. Personally, although I do like to keep an eye on the still head temperature, I prefer to check the ABV of the emerging distillate fairly often with an alcohol refractometer. This instrument is handy because it requires only a couple of drops of distillate to work. With small batches like mine, the ABV in a spirit run can change very quickly, so the ease and speed of using the refractometer is practical.

Since I did not have an experienced distiller looking over my shoulder while I was learning, I did find it helpful, during spirit runs, to divide the distillate into several small batches as it came off the still. This makes it possible to learn to smell and taste the distillate to judge the begin- and end-cuts. Believe me, it can be difficult to manage this when everything is happening so rapidly.

Here's how to do it. Ideally you will have 8 to 10 small glass containers of the same size; I use plain shot glasses that I picked up at a thrift store. You should also have three larger glass receptacles on hand to empty the small glasses into. One of these will be marked "heads," one "hearts" and one "tails."

You might be surprised at how relatively slowly the distillate comes out of the still. It may be a thin but more or less steady stream, or it may be a fairly fast drip; it doesn't gush out by the pint. I find it easy to smell and taste the distillate in each shot glass while the next is filling. If I decide, for example, that I'm still tasting heads, I empty

Graduated cylinders (250 ml and 500 ml) are very handy in the stillhouse.

I have two graduated cylinders from a laboratory supply company. One is 1 cup (250 ml), the other 2 cups (500 ml). As I got better at distinguishing the smell and taste of the distillate, I stopped using the shot glasses and began using the cylinders to collect the distillate. When one fills up, I put the other under the still and empty the full one into the appropriate heads, hearts or tails jug. This also helps me keep track accurately of how much of each I collect.

that glass in to the "heads" container, then put the empty glass back in the line of glasses.

It is interesting to me that many commercial distillers, with all the latest equipment and technical know-how and experience, still rely on their sense of smell and taste to ultimately decide when to make the cuts. So much of distilling is science, and yet so much de-

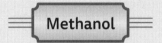

Methanol

Caution: Some recent books aimed at home or hobby distillers suggest that you simply discard the first tablespoon of "heads" for each gallon of mash you are distilling. The theory is evidently that most or all of the methanol in the wash will be concentrated in this spoonful of distillate. Some writers justify this procedure by claiming that the reports of people going blind from home-distilled liquor are greatly exaggerated. The culprit in cases of blindness is methanol, which, in quantity, can indeed cause blindness by destroying the optic nerve.

One book went on to say that if you follow this advice and get a raging headache from your finished spirit, you ought to increase the amount of "heads" you discard next time! I think this is, at best, lazy, and at worst, dangerous.

It is true that, in small batches, the amount of methanol is small. Think about this: Beer is made in much the same way as whiskey, minus the distilling. There are trace amounts of methanol present, but obviously not enough to cause any damage when consumed in moderation. However, once that wash has been distilled, the methanol, like the ethanol, has been concentrated in a much smaller volume of liquid.

My advice is to take the time to do a beer-stripping run first. Then, learn to accurately and consistently make the begin-cut in your spirit runs. Trust me, it seems unbelievably complicated at first, but with time and practice, you will get it! Not only will you minimize the risk of raging headaches and other health issues, the quality of the spirits you produce will improve as well. Plus this fascinating hobby will be a lot more fun, and why bother if it isn't fun?

pends on the kind of liquor being made, and what result the distiller is aiming for from any particular batch. To me, this was actually encouraging to learn, because it meant that, even without fancy modern equipment, I can learn the art of distilling myself.

Judging the Cuts: Different Methods

There are three basic ways to determine when to make the cuts during a spirit run: still head temperature, measuring the ABV of the distillate or smell and taste.

A number of variables can influence the still head temperature, so I don't recommend relying solely on that as a guide to making the begin- and end-cuts. It's also not that easy to keep an eye on the thermometer (which, in my case, is well above my eye level) and the distillate at the same time. However, checking the still head temperature can definitely alert you as to the approaching phase changes, so don't ignore it altogether, especially when you're learning to judge the cuts.

If you use the same formula and quantity of low wines, it is possible to have a consistent process and result. For example: Say you start with a low wine of 25% ABV. You make the begin-cut when the distillate reaches 80% ABV, with a still head temperature of about 82°C/180°F. The end-cut is made when the distillate is at 65% ABV and the still head temperature is 94°C/201°F. However…straight malt wash might have an end-cut closer to 60% ABV. A different type of still with the same wash might have the begin-cut around 72% ABV, or the end-cut at 59% ABV or even a bit lower. So, the most reliable way to judge the cuts ultimately is by smell and taste. In fact, commercial distillers, with all their modern technology and know-how, most often make the final determination of cuts by smelling and tasting.

The first distillate coming off the still has a strong solvent-like smell usually compared to nail-polish remover. Gradually this smell fades, and the first hint of whiskey taste appears. This flavor will become stronger and more concentrated as the begin-cut (the change from heads to hearts) approaches. The hearts cut should be made when this flavor is apparent but still increasing in intensity.

As the hearts run continues, the intense whiskey flavor begins to fade into a smooth, sweet taste that will continue for most of the hearts phase. When this flavor starts to lose its sweetness and you notice a hint of a harsh, bitter taste, this alerts you that the tails cut is approaching. This bitterness will increase throughout the tails run. A small amount of this bitterness is acceptable in some whiskey types, but you should make the tails cut before too much of it is allowed into the hearts receiver.

Tails are collected until the distillate is down to about 10% ABV; the still head temperature will be 97°–98°C/206°–208°F. The tails can then be added to the heads container and marked "Feints." These feints should be saved and added to future spirit runs (more about this later). As the quantity of feints naturally increases over time, some distillers periodically do a special spirit run using the feints alone. Reusing the feints not only enables the distiller to avoid wasting the residual alcohol left over from the spirit runs; re-distilling the feints tends to produce a whiskey of very rich flavor, due to the abundance of flavorful congeners present, which are further concentrated with each additional spirit run.

Feints can also be used in a pure-ethanol spirit run; this results in a very pure, neutral spirit that can be used for vodka or gin.

If you miss the begin-cut (the transition from heads to hearts), you can empty the heads container back into the still and start over. I recommend turning the heat down a bit the second time around; this will slow the process down slightly and may make it easier for you to make the cut.

Using the Fractionating Still
As If It Were a Pot Still

As mentioned before, with this kind of still, it's possible to vary the amount of separation in the emerging spirit, depending on what kind of spirit you are making. This can be accomplished two ways. One method is to increase the reflux ratio by varying the flow rate using the needle valve; this is typically done when making more high-proof, neutral spirits such as vodka or gin.

Why You Should Never Freeze-distill Liquor

You may have read about colonists and homesteaders in New England making their own freeze-distilled applejack or apple "brandy." Every year when the apples were harvested, most of the crop was promptly made into hard cider. Partly this was a means of preserving the harvest, but cider was also often the drink of choice in rural areas where the local water supply wasn't trusted. Freeze-distilling became a popular method of concentrating the hard cider into a stronger alcoholic drink.

The principle involved in freeze-distilling is simple. Containers of the cider were left outside overnight during the cold winter months. The water in the cider would freeze, and the farmer would simply remove the layer of ice from the cider in the morning before it could warm up and melt. This process was often repeated, each time resulting in a potion of higher alcoholic content.

What's wrong with this? Well, remember that all that is being removed by this process is *water*. All those other impurities that you've been learning to remove during distillation (such as methanol) are still in there. It's true that, in small quantities, there may not be enough methanol or acetaldehydes to actually harm you, but I doubt the homesteaders of the time were noted for moderation in their drinking habits. Even if the "worst" thing that happens is you suffer a raging headache the next day, honestly now, why take the chance? You've come this far in your understanding of the process of making top-quality distilled liquor; don't be tempted to take shortcuts now.

In the other method, the fractionating still can actually function more like a pot still, which requires much less reflux action during distillation. In this case, the needle valve is left wide open, and the flow rate is instead controlled by adjusting the heat source. The result is that virtually all of the condensed vapors exit the still, rather than returning to the column (reflux). In essence, this is how a pot still operates. This method works very well for making flavor-positive spirits such as whiskey or fruit brandies.

Feints

Every time you distill a batch of liquor, you will have heads and tails left over after your spirit runs. These are usually combined, and the resulting mixture is called "feints." It is useful to recycle some of the feints in subsequent spirit runs by adding a certain amount to the low wines. Not only does this enable you to recover some of the ethanol separated from the hearts during the spirit run, it also contributes esters, acetaldehydes and other elements affecting the body and flavor of the spirit. Especially in whiskey production, commercial distillers routinely add a specific proportion of feints before a spirit run. In addition, occasionally the distiller will do a special spirit run using only the feints; some claim this is the richest, most flavorful whiskey of all.

I encourage you to experiment with the amount of feints you add to your spirit runs. Be sure to record the amount of low wines and the amount of feints in each spirit run, so you can compare results later and make adjustments. I typically add about 4 liters of feints to 11 liters of low wines when making whiskey (15 liters being the maximum amount put into the still), but I do a lot of experimenting with the percentage of feints.

The Proof Hydrometer

Another useful tool is a proof hydrometer. It is similar to the hydrometer used to measure the specific gravity of mash or wort, except that it measures the alcohol content and the proof of distilled spirits. The proof hydrometer is calibrated based on the assumption that the liquid being tested contains ethanol and water and nothing else. It can't be used to measure the alcohol content of beer, mash or any undistilled alcohol, because they contain sugars, acids and other elements that influence the specific gravity.

Proof hydrometers are usually calibrated to 20°C/68°F. Ethanol expands when it is heated, so even a small variation in the temperature of the sample can change the ABV or proof reading. If your sample is not at 20°C/68°F, use the Proof Hydrometer Correction Table that came with your hydrometer to accurately determine the alcohol content.

I really like the accuracy and ease of use of the proof hydrometer for measuring the ABV of low wines and finished spirits. However, I prefer the alcohol refractometer for measuring the output of the still during spirit runs, as it automatically compensates for temperature variations and only requires a few drops to work.

Low wines of 40% ABV or more will dissolve acrylic! Be aware that some common brewing equipment such as siphon starters and hydrometer test cylinders are often made of acrylic. This isn't an issue with your mash or the fermented wort before it's distilled. The 1-cup (250 ml) graduated Pyrex cylinder I use to catch the output of my still is just the right size to use with my proof hydrometer when measuring the ABV of low wines, hearts, etc.

What About All That Water?

Very little seems to be written or discussed about the water in the condensing system, but I think it's worth taking some time to consider. It's often taken for granted that you will connect a garden hose to the condenser, turn it on and just let it go. You will need to run the water continuously for two hours or more; how long depends on the amount of wash you're distilling, and whether it is a stripping run or spirit run. That's a lot of water!

If you live in the city or somewhere with a more or less unlimited supply of water, it's easy to take it for granted. Many hobby distillers simply let the cooling water run out onto the ground as it exits the condenser coil. Why not? Water is cheap, right?

I found I spent a lot of time figuring out the condenser part of the system. Our water supply comes from three wells next to a spring-fed pond. The water is pumped from the well to a holding tank on

What Do You Do with the Liquid Left in the Still after a Distilling Run?

So I've just completed a beer-stripping run on a 15-liter batch of rum and collected about 3 liters of low wines. What do I do with the other 12 liters left in the still?

There is some alcohol in this liquid (called backset), but not a lot. With rum especially, which I make using organic blackstrap molasses, I like to use the backset to mix with the grains we feed our poultry. They absolutely love the taste, and molasses provides iron and other trace minerals and nutrients. I'm careful not to use too much of it at once, though; the backset is acidic, and too high a proportion of it in the feed is not always palatable. Plus, I'm not someone who thinks it's particularly funny to feed alcohol to

animals to see what happens. I mix in just enough to moisten the feed, and that's it.

I also save a small amount (a 1-quart Mason jar or two) to add to my next batch of mash. You may remember from the chapter on mashing that backset can be used to lower the pH of the mash water before adding the grains. To me it makes sense to use backset for this rather than citric or tartaric acid, so I do try to plan things so I have some backset on hand.

Be aware, though, that backset is fairly perishable, so if you want to save it for any length of time, you'll want to freeze it. Our freezer is so small that this isn't practical for me, so most of my backset either is mixed with feed or added to our compost.

a nearby hill and gets to the house by gravity feed. My stillhouse is located far enough from our house that it isn't practical to run a long hose to the still. Also, if I'm running water through a hose, the rest of the water system has very little pressure until I'm done. For example, we wouldn't be washing dishes, taking a shower or filling poultry drinkers while the still was running. I suppose I could get around this difficulty by only running the still in the middle of the night, but . . . maybe not.

My solution is to use a small DC-powered water pump. My condenser is the heat-exchanger type, meaning the cooling water circulates through a copper coil inside an open-ended copper pipe. The pump sits in a large bucket of cold water and is connected to the condenser coil with vinyl tubing. One tube carries cooling water to the coil intake; the other takes output water back to the bucket.

I had to do a lot of experimenting to get this system working really efficiently. At first, I had a second bucket collecting the output, because the water tended to be fairly warm after going through the coil in contact with the hot vapor. I wasn't wasting the water, though; once the distilling run was finished, I simply let the water cool off overnight to be reused another day.

Eventually I figured out that if I turn down the heat just slightly once the low wines start to drip, the output water remained cool. Again, this means the process takes a little more time, but it means I can use the same cooling water continuously. With my system, 3 to 4 gallons of cold water is plenty for a 3-hour distillation run.

When using a small pump like mine rather than a hose, be sure the pump has adequate lift power to push the water through your condenser. My pump has a maximum lift of 8 feet, plenty for my setup.

This pump cost about $10 from an eBay seller. As I said, I spent a lot of time brainstorming this part of my system. I'm still tweaking details occasionally, but overall I'm quite happy with how it works. And I'm very pleased to have a cooling system that is efficient and doesn't waste water.

Inexpensive DC-powered water pump recirculates cooling water through the condenser.

There is no electricity at my stillhouse (yet), so you might be wondering how I power that pump. I used 18-gauge automotive wiring to connect the pump leads to a 12-volt deep-cycle battery (remember, this is a DC pump). I keep the battery charged between uses with a small solar panel. The doors of my stillhouse face east, so it's convenient to charge the battery with the morning sun. The pump isn't much bigger than a golf ball, and draws very little power.

Boiling Points of Elements in Low Wines

Compound	°C	°F
Acetaldehyde	20.2	68.36
Ether	35	95
Acetone	56.6	133.88
Methanol	64.6	148.28
Acetate	77.5	171.5
Ethanol	**78.3**	**172.94**
Water	100	212
Fusel oil	80–160	176–320
Acetic acid	118	244.4

Rum

Dark rum was the first distilled spirit I attempted to make. It's David's favorite kind of liquor, and he is fond of adding it to his morning hot cocoa (see recipe on page 150), as well as in classic drinks like the Cuba Libre (see recipe on page 167). To tell the truth, one of the reasons I started with rum is because I wasn't very confident at the time about my mashing skills, and I had learned that making rum mainly involved dissolving molasses in hot water, then fermenting and distilling it. How hard could it be, right?

I was fortunate to obtain organic blackstrap molasses at whole-sale prices through our chef friend Gabriel. It comes in a bucket of a little over 50 pounds, and my records indicate that one such bucket produced about 11 bottles of beautiful, flavorful rum at 40% ABV.

 ## Rum (Master Recipe)

- 0.5 gallon (2 L) molasses (sweet or blackstrap molasses, but make sure it's unsulphured)
- 2.6 gallons (10 L) hot tap water
- 1.3 gallons (5 L) cold tap water
- 1 ounce (30 ml) distiller's yeast or 1 package distiller's yeast/ enzyme combination

Pour the molasses into a clean fermenting bucket. Add the hot tap water and stir until the molasses is dissolved. Add the cold tap water and stir well. I find that after I add the cold water, the wash is usually 32°C/90°F, just about the right temperature to add the yeast. (Be sure to check the temperature of the wash before adding the yeast, though; the temperature of hot tap water can vary.) Check and record the specific gravity of the wash; this concentration of molasses typically gives me an OG of 1.060. Stir in the yeast. Put the lid on the bucket, add cool water to your airlock and put the airlock in place. Label the lid with the contents and the date. Ferment 48 to 72 hours in a warm place; the fermentation should have slowed way down by the third day.

Since I ferment the wash in my house and distill in the stillhouse, I like to carry the fermenting bucket to the stillhouse the day before I plan to distill it. This gives the wash a chance to settle after being jostled around and mixed up a bit en route. Then I siphon the liquid off the yeast sediment into the still. Before I put the lid back on the boiling pot, I calculate the alcohol content of the wash and record that number.

Distilling Rum

Do a beer-stripping run first. Record the quantity and ABV of the low wines collected. When you are ready to do your spirit run, make sure the needle valve of the still is wide open. I like to distill rum using the pot-still method (see chapter 10), which results in a rum of deeply satisfying flavor and body.

I have gotten the best results when I collect the heads until the distillate is down to 80% ABV. Switch to the hearts and collect them until the distillate is down to 65% ABV. The second time I distilled rum, I tried waiting to make the end-cut until the distillate

My first bottle of homemade rum! It's worth investing in nice labels.

Different Kinds of Rum

As I mentioned, David prefers dark rum. It does have a lot more flavor than light rum. Light rum actually is a light, fairly neutral spirit similar to vodka. That explains why light rum is called for in a lot of cocktail recipes; like vodka, light rum won't compete with the flavors of other ingredients.

was down to 60% ABV. Everything else about the batch was exactly the same as the first, except for the end-cut, but the resulting spirit was noticeably different—not in a good way. It's hard to describe the change accurately, but to me the flavor was somehow "thinner" and seemed to be missing some of the deep caramel tones so evident in the first batch. In addition, a couple of people who drank some of this second batch reported having a bit of a headache the next day! Not good at all.

So take my advice, don't be greedy and try to get just a little bit more out of that hearts run. Do experiment with small batches and be sure to keep detailed records of what you did and what the results were. Oh, and keep in mind that you may get somewhat different results with your still than I get with mine; you may also find that using a different type of yeast makes a big difference. Play with it and have fun, but do keep those records. You'll be glad you did.

Since this was the first thing I ever distilled, I had no idea what I was doing as far as aging it. I did my best to char some oak chips (see sidebar on page 134), took a guess at how much to put in the jar with the rum, and then took more guesses as far as how long to let it sit in there. I left it for about three months, after which it was a beautiful golden color, and had an aroma reminiscent of a honey-scented whiskey. It was so smooth it was lovely to just sip on its own.

Beginner's luck, no doubt, but I have to admit it did bolster my confidence heading into the next project.

Variation: Spiced Rum

I'm not so sure I've ever even tasted spiced rum before, but I'm about to in a few days when I'm finished making a batch of this. I tend to stick with a particular liquor when I find one I like, when I should be more adventurous and try new things more often. Researching this book is certainly a good excuse!

- 1 750-milliliter (26 oz.) bottle of aged rum (I suggest dark rum, although not really dark or "black" rums)
- 1 whole nutmeg
- 1 cinnamon stick, broken into pieces
- 1 vanilla bean, split lengthwise
- 2 whole cloves
- 1 cardamom pod
- 4 black peppercorns

What About Sorghum Syrup?

As with whiskey and other spirits, in the United States rum is (yawn) defined by law: "Rum is an alcohol distillate from the fermented juice of sugar cane, sugar cane syrup, sugar cane molasses, or other sugar cane by-products…" followed by technical stuff about distilling the spirit. So, if it's not made from some kind of sugar-cane derivative like molasses, it can't be legally labeled "rum." Keeping in mind Washington's rule about ingredients being sourced in-state, this got me wondering. I mean, I was making rum with molasses, and as far as I know, our lovely state is not known for sugar-cane production. Which led me to thinking about using sorghum syrup instead, although somehow I doubt that much sorghum is grown here either. For some reason I still haven't gotten around to doing anything about it, but I would like to distill sorghum syrup sometime and see what happens.

- 1 star anise
- 3 allspice berries
- 1 large navel orange

Place the whole nutmeg in an old pillowcase or wrap loosely in a clean kitchen towel and give it a firm whack with a hammer or mallet. Put the nutmeg and all the other spices in a heavy-bottomed sauté pan. Lightly toast spices over medium-high heat until fragrant, about 2 minutes. Remove from the heat and set aside to cool. Transfer them to a blade grinder and pulse around three to four times.

Using a peeler, zest the orange, taking care to avoid any white pith. Put the zest in a 1-quart Mason jar and add the rum and toasted spices. Put the lid on securely, shake to blend and let it sit for at least 24 hours.

Strain the spiced rum, first through a strainer, then through cheesecloth or a coffee filter. Pour into a clean glass jar or bottle and label.

Gin

When I was starting to learn about distilling, one of the first things I thought about making was gin. I had only a hazy idea, at the time, of how gin was made, and no idea at all about what grains were used to make it. Then there are the juniper berries and other flavoring ingredients, referred to on gin bottle labels as "botanicals." The more I read about gin, the more intimidated I began to feel. Compared to making whiskey or rum, the process of making gin seemed complicated and a bit mysterious.

Genever, Juniper: Making Genever-style Gin

When I finally did get around to trying it, I decided to begin with genever-style gin. Although it is a multi-step process involving several distillation runs, for some reason it appealed to me as a place to start.

Genever is the Dutch word for "juniper," the evergreen shrub whose aromatic berries supply the dominant flavor of gin. Traditionally, genever is distilled to a lower proof than London dry gin; it is also usually lightly sweetened. The two main styles of genever are oude (old) and jonge (young). These terms refer not to the age of the spirit but to the recipes used: oude is the old or traditional recipe, and jonge is the more modern recipe. As in the United States and

Canada, the ingredients used and the alcohol content are defined by law. Dutch law also specifies the level of sweetening that is acceptable in different types of genever.

Genever was originally created around 1650 by a Dutch doctor, Franciscus de la Boë. It was promoted as a medicinal tonic; juniper berries were well-known even then for their diuretic properties. Genever quickly became popular outside of Holland, particularly in England, where its use as a beverage soon outgrew its medicinal use. By the early 1700s, the more full-bodied, slightly sweet genever was changing in England to a lighter, cleaner style that became known as London dry gin. This style, still the most widely known gin type, is much closer to a neutral spirit than traditional genever, as it is distilled to a higher proof.

Compared with London dry gin, the process of making genever is unique. London dry gin is typically made from a mash of wheat or rye, while genever utilizes corn, rye and malted barley. The fermented mash is then distilled twice to make a "malt wine," a full-bodied spirit not unlike malt whiskey. The malt wine is then steeped with juniper berries and other botanicals and then redis-

My first batch of genever in process.

tilled. This results in a complex and very interesting gin. Some genevers are then aged in barrels, increasing the smoothness and flavor profile.

Just reading through the process of making genever, it sounds like a labor of love. Some low-quality mass-market gins are made by simply mixing extracts of juniper berries and other botanicals with a base spirit (a neutral spirit similar to vodka). Top-quality gins are distilled at least three times; during distillation, the vapors rise through a special basket that holds the botanicals, picking up the flavors and resulting in a subtle and complex gin. Genever is usually distilled to 72 to 80 proof (36% to 40% ABV), while London dry gins are typically distilled to 80 proof or more.

When I made my first batch of genever, I decided from the start not to sweeten it. The addition of sugar, along with the fuller body of the malt wine-based spirit, has given genever the reputation of not being recommended for mixed drinks. Being a fan of the classic Gin & Tonic myself, I decided to try to make a genever-style gin that would lend itself easily to the G & T, and maybe even a martini.

Step by Step: Genever-style Gin

- 4.2 gallons (16 L) of water
- 4.4 pounds (2 kg) cracked corn
- 4.4 pounds (2 kg) malted barley
- 4.4 pounds (2 kg) rye (malted or unmalted)
- 1 gallon (4 L) of water
- 2 tablespoons (30 ml) distilling yeast
- 1 to 1½ tablespoons (15 to 20 ml) of lightly crushed juniper berries

1. Heat 4.2 gallons of water to 74°C/165°F.
2. Stir in grains, cover and hold for 30 minutes.
3. Heat 1 gallon of water to about 93°C/200°F and add to mash pot, stirring well.
4. Cover and hold for about 1 hour, stirring occasionally.
5. Increase temperature of mash to 72°C/162°F, stirring frequently. Cover and hold 30 minutes.
6. Strain liquid from grains into fermenting bucket.
7. Cool liquid to about 28°C/82°F.
8. Pitch yeast (I used 2 tablespoons distilling yeast) and ferment.

Distillation

1. Transfer wash to still, keeping back as much of the yeast slurry as possible.
2. Do a stripping run, aiming for a distillate of about 30% ABV.
3. Redistill low wines to about 46% to 48% ABV.
4. Divide malt wine into four equal volumes (I used quart Mason jars).
   a. Part one stays pure malt wine.
   b. Part two is redistilled to 75% ABV.
   c. Part three: Add lightly crushed juniper berries to the jar. Let soak 2 to 3 days and then redistill.
   d. Part four: Grind and add remaining botanicals (below) to the jar, let soak 2 to 3 days and then redistill.

Botanicals

- 3 tablespoons (10 g) juniper berries
- 1½ teaspoons (5 g) coriander seed
- 1 teaspoon (2 g) wormwood
- 1 teaspoon (2 g) angelica root
- 2 teaspoons hops (4 g) or 1 teaspoon (2 g) if pelletized
  (I used homegrown East Kent Goldings hops)
- ¾ teaspoon (2 g) caraway seed
- 1 teaspoon (2 g) each: lemon peel, orange peel
- ½ teaspoon each: lavender flowers and lemon grass
- ¼ teaspoon (1 g) each: nutmeg, cinnamon, cubeb, grains of paradise, anise seed, peppercorns, orris root

5. Combine all four volumes of malt wine.

This large, heavy mortar and pestle makes quick work of grinding spices.

At this point, I thought the aroma of the genever was very pleasant but not strongly aromatic. I redistilled the spirit one more time in my small essential-oil

Distill your genever one more time for a drier, London-style gin.

distiller, adding juniper berries and lemon and orange peel to the steam chamber above the boiling pot.

This additional distilling run further concentrated the flavors and resulted in a smoother, higher-proof spirit. I then poured it into a half-gallon Mason jar, diluted it to 40% ABV and added a couple of handfuls of lightly toasted American oak chips to the jar. Then I waited, quite impatiently, for the recommended 3 to 4 weeks before tasting my creation.

I will soon be harvesting juniper berries for making gin.

Other Uses for All Those Interesting Botanicals

I was so excited getting ready to make my first batch of gin, I went a little crazy buying herbs and spices. One day I looked up and found I had more than half a gallon of this, three pounds of that. Oops.

I figured, stored in airtight jars, it's not like the things were going to go bad anytime soon. I did start thinking about what else I might use them for, though. One obvious choice is to make homemade bitters (see chapter 20). The other thing I thought of was using them to concoct herbal remedies. I picked up a good book on the subject. Soon I was having even more fun in my stillhouse, formulating infusions and salves among other things.

The point is, plan ahead, be creative, and be thrifty! Don't just do like I did and go wild buying up a lot of stuff before you think about what it will be used for (not to mention how and where it will be stored). But be warned: This kind of thing can be addictive.

After all that work, I had finally gotten over my initial timidity about making gin. And, oh boy, did I enjoy my first Gin & Tonic, made with my first batch of gin! It definitely has a stronger juniper flavor than a lot of gins, and might not be to everyone's taste in a mixed drink. Personally I think the key is balance: use the right amount of tonic water (see Recipe on page 166). In a later chapter, I'll walk you through the process of making your own tonic water.

I'll keep working on my genever recipe and techniques, but overall I'm very pleased with the results from my first attempt at making gin.

Vodka

When I first started learning to distill, I didn't really think I was going to be making vodka. This might sound odd, since I chose to build the type of still particularly suited to distilling spirits like gin and vodka. It's just that I wanted to make dark rum for David and, you know, all that other stuff for me. I didn't often have cocktails made with vodka, at least not until I recently "discovered" the joys of the Cosmopolitan. Also I was intimidated by the process, like I was with gin. So anyway, vodka was way down there on the priority list.

Around that time, I was in a liquor store in Portland, Oregon, with my sister. She was looking for a bottle of vodka to use in making limoncello. We faced an astounding selection of vodkas, some on shelves too high to reach. They were expensive and cheap, domestic and foreign, made from grain or made from potatoes, even a few locally made "craft" vodkas. I don't remember which brand she ended up choosing, but it did get me wondering: What (if anything) is the difference between one vodka and another?

It seemed to me that, other than price and bottle design (some were quite elaborate), there wasn't much to point you toward one over the other. What I didn't know at the time was that the US government, bless its meddlesome little heart, defines such things as vodka and other commercially produced spirits. The legal definition of vodka is: "Vodka is neutral spirits so distilled, or so treated after distillation with charcoal or other materials, as to be without distinctive character, aroma, taste or color."

So, thought I, if vodka by definition is basically a neutral spirit, there really isn't any difference between one and another. Obviously I had more to learn. It's more or less true of American-made vodkas, although there is some variation in the proof (alcohol content) of vodkas. Vodkas produced outside the United States can vary a lot. Russian vodkas, for example, are usually made from grain (typically rye), while Polish vodkas are more often made from potatoes. Still others are made primarily from wheat. In any case, European, Russian and Scandinavian vodkas can have a lot more character than American types.

To make matters more confusing, there are other ways vodkas can differ from one another. Here's where you'll have to read labels. Most kinds of vodka are distilled at least three times; some opt for a fourth distillation run. Almost all commercial vodkas are charcoal-filtered at least once, while some are filtered three or more times. A few proudly declare they are filtered through exotic materials like diamond dust. I must be getting cynical in my old age, but somehow I suspect that this does more to justify the price tag than to further purify the spirit.

If you're going to buy or make vodka, first consider what you're going to use it for. Most Americans prefer American vodkas for making mixed drinks, because the neutral taste doesn't compete with the taste of other ingredients. European and Russian vodkas are great to sip chilled on their own. If you're planning to make bitters or infusions, a higher-proof vodka is best.

Now, on to making vodka! Among craft distilleries in America, more vodka is produced than any other spirit, by a long way. No doubt this is partly due to the fact that vodka is rarely aged at all before being sold. It's a good way for new distillers to get a product on the market quickly and start recovering some of their start-up costs. Again, the popularity of vodka for use in mixed drinks also helps.

There are at least a couple of ways to make vodka on a small scale. If you have a pot still, your best bet is to follow a grain-based recipe like those below. Then you will need to distill your spirit at least three times, since pot stills are a lot less efficient than column stills. I suggest you try this only after you have some experience doing spirit runs and are comfortable using a refractometer; on the second and third distillation runs, the alcohol content of the spirit will increase, and it's important to be able to accurately separate the hearts from the heads and tails.

If you have a column or fractionating still, you may be able to distill a fairly pure, high-proof vodka in two runs. Whatever you may have read elsewhere, I strongly recommend (once again) starting with a stripping run and then doing a fairly slow, careful spirit run.

Another way to make vodka starts with the assumption that you have done a number of spirit runs and have saved the feints (the heads and tails mixed together) from those runs. You can simply redistill the feints to a high proof; this means at least one run in a column still and probably two runs in a pot still. This method, of which I highly approve because it minimizes waste, is outlined in detail in *Making Pure Corn Whiskey* (see Books in Appendix A). It is the method I have used most often for making vodka, with excellent results.

After distilling, you will probably want to filter your vodka. Filtering is discussed in chapter 18.

So you're ready to make some vodka. First I offer a recipe (with some misgivings) for "sugar-shine," as it is popularly called. This is the only recipe in this book that I have not actually tried. I include it here because I get asked about it a lot. Frankly, I'm not crazy about it. It's not an economical way to make vodka or anything else. I suspect its popularity arises from the theory that you start with a sugary liquid of high specific gravity, ferment it with a highly alcohol-tolerant Turbo yeast and end up with a wash of 40% alcohol or even more. Supposedly this enables you to distill a passable spirit in just one run, since it already has so much alcohol in it.

Caution: This method assumes you have a column still and know how to use it.

See the sidebar on page 56 for more discussion on sugar washes and why grain mashes are preferable.

Sugar-shine

- 6 gallons (23 L) unchlorinated or filtered water
- 14 pounds (6.4 kg) granulated white sugar
- 1 package Turbo yeast (enough for at least 6 gallons wash)

In a large stock pot or mashing pot (at least 4-gallon capacity), bring 2 gallons of water to a boil. Turn off heat, add the sugar and stir to dissolve. Put 3 gallons of cold water in a fermenting bucket (8 gallons or larger), then pour in the hot water and sugar mixture. Stir to combine. Check temperature; you are aiming for about 38°C/100°F. Add more warm or cold water until there is a total of 6.6 gallons liquid (25 liters). Check temperature again. If it is over 38°C/100°F,

Sugar-shine and Flavorings

Some recent books advocate making this sugar wash, distilling it and then adding flavor essences to "create" the kind of spirit you want. (People often come up after presentations and tell me enthusiastically about this way of making spirits.) So you would presumably use something like Essence of Malt Whiskey or Pure Rum Flavoring. Maybe it works just fine. I just hope you won't be too disappointed if I don't tell you how to do it. First of all, I haven't done this myself, and second, this book is about making really high-quality spirits, and doing it economically. One of these days, I will try this recipe myself, just because I'm curious as to the yield and cost.

just put the fermenter lid on loosely and let it cool down a bit. Check the specific gravity and record this number.

Add the yeast and stir vigorously until the yeast and nutrients are dissolved. Put on the lid, add the airlock and let it ferment at room temperature. Depending on conditions, fermentation times can vary, so remember to watch the airlock for bubbling. Once the bubbling slows down noticeably, start checking the specific gravity once a day. Once fermentation is complete, check and record the specific gravity. Transfer the wash to the still with a siphon, leaving behind as much yeast sediment as possible. Record the volume of wash in the still and estimated alcohol content. Distill in a column still.

Grain-based Vodka

OK, now for the good stuff. Here is a typical grain-based vodka recipe. I've used wheat here, but you can try substituting rye malt for some of the grain. You should be able to find wheat malt and flaked wheat at your local homebrew shop.

Wheat Vodka

- 6 gallons (23 L) filtered or unchlorinated water
- 1½ teaspoons (7.5 ml) gypsum
- 8½ pounds (3.9 kg) flaked wheat
- 2.2 pounds (1 kg) wheat malt, crushed
- 1 package whiskey yeast/enzyme combination

Have two large (at least 8-gallon capacity) fermenting buckets on hand.

Pour all the water into a large stockpot; I use my stainless steel 10-gallon mashing pot for this. Heat the water to 71°C/160°F. Stir in the gypsum, then add the flaked wheat. Stir until the grain begins to liquefy; it will look something like oatmeal. The temperature will drop when you add the grain, so check it again. If it is below 67°C/152°F, heat gently until the temperature is between 67°–68°C/152°–155°F. Be sure to stir while it is heating. If the temperature is above 68°C/155°F, stop and let it cool until it is 68°C/155°F.

Add the wheat malt, stirring to incorporate. Put the lid on the pot and let the mash rest for 60 minutes. Stir gently and check the temperature every 15 minutes or so; it should stay at 65°C/149°F or above. After 60 minutes, use the iodine test to check for starch conversion. If conversion isn't complete, replace the lid and let rest another 30 minutes.

Let the mash cool to 32°C/90°F. Take a sample of the clear liquid on top of the mash and test the specific gravity. Record this number; it should be about 1.060 to 1.065 (remember to correct for temperature). Transfer mash, with the grain, to a fermenting bucket. Pour the mash vigorously back and forth between the two buckets several times to aerate the mash. Add the yeast, put the lid and airlock on the fermenter, and let ferment in a warm place until fermentation is done.

Strain the grains from the mash using a large straining bag. (See chapter 8 for information on feeding the mashed grains to your poultry or other livestock.) Let the strained liquid stand for several hours or overnight to let the yeast sediment settle.

Siphon the wash to the still. Be sure to record the volume of liquid, specific gravity and estimated alcohol content of the wash. Distill at least 3 times, starting with a stripping run.

Flavored Vodkas

These are fun to experiment with. One I haven't tried yet is an infusion of fresh horseradish in vodka; seems this is quite the thing for making Bloody Marys. I started growing horseradish about a year ago, and it's got a nice hot horseradish flavor, so it should work well for infusions. I'd also like to make a black pepper-infused vodka. Here are a couple of recipes to get you started.

Aquavit

- 50 ounces (1.5 L) good-quality vodka
- 3 tablespoons (45 ml) caraway seed
- 2 tablespoons (30 ml) cumin seed
- 2 tablespoons (30 ml) dill seed
- 1 tablespoon (15 ml) fennel seed
- 1 tablespoon (15 ml) coriander seed
- 2 whole star anise
- 3 whole cloves
- Peel of ½ organic lemon, cut in strips
- Peel of ½ organic orange, cut in strips
- 1 ounce (30 ml) simple syrup (optional)

Preheat your oven to 204°C/400°F. Toast the seeds on a foil-lined cookie sheet for 6 to 8 minutes; stir 2 or 3 times while they are toasting. Remove from oven and let cool briefly. Crush seeds lightly in a mortar and pestle, then put them in a large infusion jar (a half-gallon Mason jar works well). Add the star anise, cloves, lemon and orange peel, then the vodka. Add a bit more vodka if needed to completely cover the other ingredients. Seal tightly with a lid and shake briefly.

Infuse at room temperature for not less than 2 weeks. Shake the jar every 2 days while infusing. Strain, first through a strainer, then through cheesecloth or a coffee filter. Add the simple syrup, if using, and bottle. Best stored in the freezer.

Making citron (lemon) vodka is easy and quick.

Citron Vodka

- 1 bottle (750 ml) filtered vodka
- ¼ cup (60 ml) dried organic lemon peel (purchased or homemade; see method below)
- Peel of 3 fresh organic lemons, cut in thin strips, with no pith

In a half-gallon Mason jar, pour vodka over lemon peel and fresh rind. Cover and let macerate for 2 days. Smell and taste and strain out lemon rind as soon as the flavor and aroma suit your taste. Perfect for making the quintessential Cosmopolitan (see recipe on page 165).

Dried Citrus Peel

If you plan to use dried citrus peel frequently, I suggest buying it in quantity. I get organic lemon, lime and orange peel by the pound at very reasonable prices from Starwest Botanicals (see Resources). For small quantities, though, it can be more cost-effective to make your own. It also gives you the choice of different types of fruit, especially with oranges, which can have bitter or sweet peel.

It's always best to buy organic citrus fruits when you plan to use the peel. Preheat your oven to its lowest setting. Using a vegetable peeler or sharp paring knife, cut thin strips of peel. Try to avoid cutting into the white pith. Cut the strips into small pieces, about ¼" by ½". It's more important that the pieces be fairly uniform in size, so don't worry about the size too much. Spread the pieces on a baking sheet in one layer. Put the sheet in the oven and bake until the peel has shrunk noticeably; if you see the edges of the pieces starting to brown, take the sheet out of the oven. Depending on the temperature in your oven, this can take anywhere from 5 minutes to 20 minutes or so. The peel will continue to dry once it's out of the oven, so put the baking sheet on a cooling rack and let it sit until the peel feels dry. It can be used right away or stored in an airtight jar.

Did you know that there actually isn't all that much difference between gin and vodka? The main thing that makes gin different is that, at one point in the distillation, a special basket containing juniper berries and various herbs and spices is placed in the still. As the spirit begins to vaporize, the steam rises up through the basket, infusing the spirit with the familiar juniper tang of gin. Without this extra step, gin would smell and taste pretty much like one more vodka.

Malt Whiskey

O thou, my Muse! Guid auld Scotch drink,
Whether thro' wimplin worms thou jink
Or, richly brown, ream owre the brink,
In glorious faem,
Inspire me, till I lisp an' wink,
To sing thy name!

[From "Good Scotch Drink" by Robert Burns]

Although I love a good Scotch whiskey, I must admit I don't drink it all that often. It's definitely the kind of thing I prefer to sip in the company of others. Believe it or not, before I met David, I'm pretty sure I had never even tasted Scotch before. I have heard it said that you either like Scotch or you like bourbon, but not both. You probably won't be surprised to learn that I do, in fact, like both. Not usually at the same time, though.

Most often, Scotch is a once-a-year treat at our house. David is a big fan of Robert Burns, the national poet of Scotland. Burns lived in the late 1700s and died before the age of forty. In addition to being a prolific poet much loved to this day, Burns was also noted for his drinking. Burns' famous poem "Tam O'Shanter" tells the memorable tale of how the narrator had been on an epic drinking binge; he is now on his way home, trying to concoct a plausible explanation for his long-suffering wife. En route, he meets the devil, and much merriment ensues. It's worth buying a book of Burns' poetry just for the poem "To a Louse." The narrator is in church, fascinated by the sight of a louse impertinently crawling on the bonnet of one of the well-dressed society ladies sitting in front of him. But I digress.

On January 25, Robert Burns' birthday, we like to invite a few friends over for a traditional Robbie Burns Day dinner. Almost traditional; I haven't actually ever made a haggis. (You had me at "sheep's stomach.") I read somewhere that roast lamb was a perfectly acceptable substitute, so that's what I do. Then there's the Neeps 'n' Tatties, a mashed blend of potatoes and turnips. Fast-forward to dessert, and enjoy a goodly portion of Tipsy Laird, a trifle-like, sponge-cake-based concoction laced with both brandy and sherry. Mm mm mmmmm. Excuse me while I go get a snack.

OK, I'm back. So after the dinner, the rest of the evening is spent sampling different single malt whiskies and taking turns reading Robbie Burns poetry while reclining in various comfortable chairs near the woodstove. If you think this is a lovely way to spend a cold winter's evening, you nailed it.

You Say Whiskey, I Say Whisky

Why are some types of whiskey spelled with the "e" while others are not? Traditionally, the Scots and Canadians use "whisky," and the Irish and Americans use "whiskey." Other than tradition, no one seems to know just why the variation exists. Personally I prefer it without the "e"; however, in this book, I have reluctantly chosen to use that other spelling, mostly because I got tired of having "whisky" flagged by that officious Word spell-check. But then, what can you expect from a spelling checker that tries to correct my maiden name and doesn't recognize household words like azeotrope? Next time I write a book, things will be different.

Single malt whiskey was one of the first things I thought about when I started learning about distilling. This was mostly because one of the two ponds on our property is a natural peat bog, quite a large one. I knew just enough at the time to know that the main difference between Scotch-style malt whiskey and any other whiskey is that Scotch whiskies get their unique smoky flavor from peat. During the malting process, the wet barley is dried over a peat fire, imbuing the grain with layers of complex smokiness. How smoky the finished product is depends on the percentage of this peated malt in the mash; some use nothing but peated malt, in others the peated malt makes up only a small proportion of the total mash bill. (Try one of the Isle of Islay malt whiskies for a really smoky dram.)

Actually I figured that I have no excuse for not making peated malt whiskey. However, I soon realized that making my own peated malt would involve first learning to make my own malted barley. I read about this process and had a go at it, using organic malting barley I bought from our friend and well-known local organic farmer, Nash Huber. I'm sure glad I started out with very small batches! It's more complicated than it might seem at first, but the first batch was the only one that didn't turn out quite well. I wasn't very organized about it, though, or I would have been prepared to dry the malt over a peat fire. This is all leading up to me confessing that all the peated malt I've used so far for making whiskey was bought from our local homebrew shop. Whew. Got that off my chest.

For single malt whiskey, it is important to have at least a small amount of peated malt in the mash, as it triggers a chemical reaction that produces characteristic honey notes in the whiskey. Don't leave it out entirely unless you are aiming for something more like a single malt Irish whiskey (which is quite delicious, by the by).

Once you've got your peated malt, mashing, fermenting and distilling malt whiskey is straightforward. Here is a typical recipe; I recommend following this recipe the first time, then experimenting with varying percentages of peated malt to find out what you like the best.

Scotch-style Malt Whiskey

Ready to taste my first malt whiskey!

- 5 gallons (19 L) filtered or unchlorinated water
- Backset or citric or tartaric acid, as needed to adjust the mash water pH (see chapter 8)
- 15 pounds (6.8 kg) malted two-row barley
- ½ pound (225 g) peated malt
- 1 package whiskey yeast with enzymes
- 2 tablespoons (30 ml) plain yogurt or dried cheesemaking culture

Put 2½ gallons of the water in an 8- or 10-gallon stockpot and heat to 71°C/160°F. Stir in the malted barley and peated malt. Hold the temperature between 67°C/152°–155°F for 90 minutes. Use the iodine test (see sidebar on page 56) to check for starch conversion. Strain the grains from the wort into an 8-gallon fermenting bucket,

Why Is It Called "Single Malt"?

At first glance, I thought this simply meant that the whiskey was made with one kind of malt. Actually, single malt by definition means a 100% malt whiskey that has been produced at one distillery.

It may be a blend of malt whiskies of different ages. If it contains whiskies from different years, though, the age statement on the bottle will refer to the youngest whiskey in the blend.

using a large straining bag. Leave the bag suspended in the fermenter. Heat 5 quarts of the remaining water to 74°C/165°F. Pour this water through the grains in the bag. Heat the remaining 5 quarts of water to 82°C/180°F and repeat the rinsing of the grains. Let the grains drain thoroughly into the fermenting bucket, then set the grains aside.

Cool the wort to 33°C/92°F. Check the specific gravity and record. Add the yeast and yogurt or cheese culture. Ferment at room

Magical, Mysterious Peat

Peat, I learned recently, is a precursor to coal. It is basically the result of many years of accumulation of decaying vegetation. In an acidic environment, with little or no drainage, the moss and plant roots and other materials slowly decompose because it never gets a chance to dry out. Over many years, the pressure of more and more plant material building up eventually results in the formation of coal, well below the surface of the Earth.

Closer to ground level, though, the decaying plant material remains relatively loose, and is easy to dig or cut from the banks of the bog. Although it is only around 60% carbon, it makes a passable fuel for burning when dried. The Scots began using peat as a fuel source when the local coal and wood supplies proved inadequate. This was another of those dis-coveries that happened by "accident"; the malt houses were drying the malt over peat fires, the aroma of which permeated the drying malt. There is a lot of scientific stuff involving phenols, chemical reactions and other things, but for now, all you need to know is that the peat smoke is responsible for the undertones of honey as well as smokiness. It's the one big difference between Scotch malt whiskies and all the other whiskies out there.

I don't know how many peat bogs there are in the Olympic Mountains, but I assume that ours is not the only one. My father's side of the family traces back to County Fife in Scotland, and the thought of making a single malt whiskey using our own homestead peat just makes me smile.

temperature for 2 to 6 days, or until fermentation has slowed considerably or stopped. Check the specific gravity again and record this number.

Transfer the wort to your still, leaving the yeast sediment in the wort. Do a stripping run first; you should have low wines around 30% ABV. Then do a spirit run, switching from heads to hearts when the emerging distillate reaches 80% ABV. Collect hearts until the emerging distillate is down to 60% to 62% ABV before switching to tails.

I like to plan single malt whiskey distillations for some time after I've been making bourbon or rum. When I strain the charred oak chips out of the aged spirit, I save the chips to use for aging malt whiskey. Of course, you can age your whiskey using freshly charred or toasted oak chips too. Part of the fun of all this is the virtually infinite range of results you can get just by tweaking one little detail of the process here or there. Remember to keep records, so when you hit on a particularly yummy formula, you can duplicate it!

Save the heads and tails from all whiskey spirit runs and mix them together in a glass jar or bottle. Add a small amount of this mixture (called "feints") to your next whiskey spirit run. This is commonly done in commercial distilleries, and is part of the mystique; somehow the added feints improve the flavor of the finished whiskey. It works just as well in small batches like this.

Irish Whiskey

I've been in a bit of an Irish whiskey rut for a while now. Poor me. I like bourbon and single malt whiskey too, but I wouldn't drink them every day. There's something about Irish whiskey, I don't know. The process of making it is very similar to that of single malt whiskey, with two main exceptions. Irish whiskey isn't made using peated malt like Scotch; it is most often a blend of malted and unmalted barley, although wheat and corn are also sometimes included in the mix. The other difference is that Irish whiskey is almost always distilled three times, compared with two distillation runs for most other kinds of whiskey.

After dark rum, which was the first thing I made because it's David's favorite (aren't I a good wife), Irish whiskey was the next thing I wanted to distill. It took me a while to get around to it, though, partly because I didn't do much distilling while I was finishing up my first book, and also I got distracted by lots of other fun distilling projects along the way.

After reading about the various grains used in making Irish whiskey, I had an idea one day. I took some COB (a mix of corn, oats and barley) from the feed shed and mashed it, adding in what I hoped was an appropriate amount of malt for starch conversion. After fermenting and distilling it and aging it several months with charred oak chips, would you believe it smelled and tasted a lot like

Irish whiskey? I swear this is true. Next time (if there is a next time), I'll triple-distill it like a proper Irish whiskey; even after aging, it still had a bit of a hard edge to it. Kind of cool, although our feed supplier might not be amused.

I just realized that as I am writing this, Happy Hour is going by fast. If I don't get my drink order in soon, I'll be paying a dime instead of a nickel. I'll be back.

Irish Whiskey

- 5 gallons (19 L) filtered or unchlorinated water
- 7½ pounds (3.4 kg) malted two-row barley, cracked
- 7½ pounds (3.4 kg) unmalted barley, cracked
- Backset or citric or tartaric acid, as needed to adjust the mash water pH (see chapter 8)
- 1 ounce (30 ml) distiller's yeast
- 2 tablespoons (30 ml) plain yogurt (optional)

Heat 2½ gallons of water to 71°C/160°F. Adjust pH if needed. Add cracked unmalted barley, then the malted barley and stir to moisten all the grain. Hold the mash temperature at 67°C/152°F for 90 minutes. Drain liquid from grains into fermenting bucket. Heat 5 quarts of water to 74°C/165°F and wash the mashed grains; drain the liquid into the fermenting bucket. Heat the remaining 5 quarts of water to 82°C/180°F and rinse the grains as before. Pour all the liquid into the fermenting bucket and mix well.

Cool to about 29°C/85°F; check and record the specific gravity. Add the yeast and the yogurt (if using). Put the lid and airlock in place and ferment in a warm spot for 72 to 96 hours.

Transfer the wash to your still and do a stripping run. Your low wines should be around 30% ABV. Do a spirit run, making the heads cut when the emerging distillate reaches 80% ABV. Switch to tails when the emerging distillate is about 55% ABV. Now do one more

What's Happening with the Irish Distilling Industry Today?

Many years ago, the distilling industry in Ireland nearly disappeared. Seems a powerful Scottish company, the Distillers Company Ltd., in a move apparently meant to enhance their dominance of Scotch whiskey in the UK, began buying up (and then closing down) Irish distilleries. On the brink of Scotland's success at this questionable maneuver, Irish Distillers Ltd. was created, in a desperate effort to save the Irish whiskey industry. This was a merger of various remaining distilleries that left only two distilleries in operation: Old Bushmills in County Antrim, and Midleton Distillery in County Cork. This kept the Irish distilling industry alive, if not thriving, for quite some time.

The Cooley Distillery, opening in 1987, was the first new Irish distillery in nearly a hundred years. In 1998, the Irish Distillers Ltd. was bought by the huge company Pernod Ricard, which then sold the Old Bushmills Distillery to the even bigger Diageo in 2005.

It has been speculated that the near-extinction of the Irish distilling industry came about largely through their own unwillingness to add the newer column stills to their distilleries, along with the traditional pot stills. Today, though, most Irish whiskies are actually a blend of column-still and pot-still whiskies, a style that has boomed in popularity in recent years. For example, the most popular brand, Jameson, is now among the top ten whiskey brands in the world, with sales of about 50 million bottles in 2013. In fact, sales of Jameson grew by an astounding 20% annually for ten years in a row!

So the good news is that the Irish whiskey industry is making a strong comeback. I read that some 15 new distilleries are planned in Ireland; current distillers are generously giving technical advice to the newcomers. For Ireland, its distillers and consumers worldwide, the future looks increasingly bright.

spirit run on the hearts from the first spirit run. Distill this run as before, but only until the accumulated hearts are between 80% to 90% ABV.

Dilute and age the whiskey according to the directions in chapter 18. Remember to save the heads and tails, mixed together in a container labeled "Whiskey Feints."

The first couple of times I tried this recipe, I ended up with a wash of about 1.050, a little on the low side. I use a 10-gallon heavy stainless steel stockpot for mashing, and I suspected that the mash temperature was dropping a little low during the 90-minute rest period. Turns out this was correct. (Plus during the winter, our kitchen tends to be on the cool side unless we have the woodstove going.) It actually helps a lot to simply wrap the pot with a thick towel. Someday I'll decide to invest in a real mash tun designed for this kind of thing. Maybe if I start dropping hints . . . after all, Christmas is only about ten months away.

Try making a single malt Irish whiskey by substituting malted barley for the unmalted barley in this recipe. Single malt Irish whiskey is usually quite a bit lighter in color than blended Irish whiskey, so try aging it with toasted but uncharred oak chips. Delicious.

Other Kinds of Whiskey

Canadian Whiskey

For many years, rye was the predominant grain used in the production of Canadian whiskey. Indeed, even today whiskey is often still referred to simply as "rye" in Canada. These days, the predominant grains used are corn and wheat.

Almost all Canadian whiskies are blends, although a few distilleries are now making a name for themselves with single malt whiskies. To date, I have not tried making a Canadian whiskey. My plan is to make a few more batches of rye whiskey (see recipe below), using various formulas, and then attempt to create my own blend.

Bourbon

This was another thing I raided the feed shed for. All those bags of lovely organic cracked corn. And it's not like it would go to waste if I used it for making bourbon; once the corn was mashed, we feed it to the chickens and turkeys and ducks. They LOVE it! And the corn is already cracked, so it's an easy thing to organize the grains to be mashed.

Basic Bourbon Recipe

- 5 gallons (19 L) filtered or unchlorinated water
- 10 pounds (4.5 kg) cracked corn
- 1¼ pounds (0.6 kg) cracked rye berries
- 1¼ pounds (0.6 kg) flaked wheat
- 2½ pounds (1.1 kg) malted barley
- 1 package whiskey yeast/enzyme combination

Heat the water in a large stockpot to 71°C/160°F. Stir in the corn, rye berries and flaked wheat, followed by the malted barley. Put the lid on the pot and hold the temperature at 66°–68°C/152°–155°F for 60 minutes. Test for starch conversion using the iodine test, and hold for up to another 60 minutes if necessary for full starch conversion.

Cool the mash to 33°C/92°F. Transfer the mash to an 8-gallon fermentation bucket. Add yeast. Ferment hot (29°–32°C/85°–90°F if possible) for 2 to 4 days. Strain the liquid from the grains. Check and record the specific gravity of the wash.

Transfer the wash to your still, including the yeast, and do a stripping run. The low wines should be about 30% ABV. Next do a spirit run, making the cut to hearts when the emerging distillate is down to 80% ABV. Distill until the accumulated hearts are between 68%–75% ABV.

Age your bourbon using heavily charred oak chips. I suggest 4 to 6 months for anything up to a gallon, maybe 2 to 3 months if you have less than half a gallon.

20-kilo (44 pound) bags of organic cracked corn for making bourbon and other whiskies.

Variations on the Bourbon Theme

Rye adds spicy notes to whiskey. To ratchet up the spice in your bourbon (known as high rye bourbon), simply increase the proportion of rye in your formula. For wheated bourbon, try replacing the

To produce the characteristic cherry-flavored esters in bourbon, you'll need to use a yeast strain known to produce this ester. Lalvin ICV-D21 is a good place to start. You might also ask your homebrew shop people for a recommendation. Once you get a sense of how many brewing yeast strains there are to choose from, you'll begin to get an inkling of just how unlimited is the potential for experimenting with distilled spirits.

rye in the basic recipe with flaked wheat. Wheat can add smoothness to whiskey, but beware of adding too much; it might tone down the bourbon character more than you wanted.

Tennessee Whiskey

Tennessee whiskey is very similar to bourbon, with one main difference: Before bottling, it is filtered through a deep bed of sugar-maple charcoal. This process, which can take a week or more, adds color and removes some of the congeners (flavor elements), resulting in a smooth, mellow taste.

At this writing, I have not tried making Tennessee whiskey, although I've made several batches of bourbon. I mention it mainly to encourage you to be creative and think of what you can do with the materials you have on hand. As far as I know, we don't have sugar maples on our property, but we do have vine maples and a lot of other deciduous and evergreen trees. For that matter, I have dry wild cherry bark in my stillhouse, patiently waiting to be used in my next batch of bitters. Maybe I'll toast some of that and use it to filter something. You never know; this is undoubtedly how a lot of famous liqueur and bitters formulas were "discovered."

Sour Mash Whiskey

This was one of the first kinds of whiskey I attempted to make. One of my books suggested that beginners (i.e., people without experience in mashing grains) start with sour mash since it doesn't involve mashing the grain. I went through the process mostly out of curiosity. Also I was still feeling intimidated about making distilled liquor, and figured I would do everything I could to make it easier on myself.

Originally, the sour mash process was meant to slow the growth of unwanted bacteria in the whiskey mash by lowering the pH before the yeast was added. Usually this was done by saving some of the previous batch of fermented mash and adding it to the next batch. This helps ensure consistency of results from one batch to the next, because some of the yeast from the first fermentation is retained for the next batch. In addition, this process can also encourage yeast to form alcohol more rapidly since it shortens the period in which the yeast is working to produce acid.

If you want to experiment with sour mash whiskey, I recommend the procedure outlined in *Making Pure Corn Whiskey* (see Books in Appendix A). It's not the quickest or cheapest way to make whiskey, but it does result in a lovely, smooth, flavorful spirit.

Hops: Good in Beer, Not So Much in Whiskey

A book I have on making Scotch ale (can I just say, yum) said that if you distilled Scotch ale, you would have whiskey. This was years ago, and might have been one of those little things that wormed its way into my subconscious brain and has been simmering on low all this time. For all I know, this was the first hint that I would turn my hand to distilling at some point in my life.

Scotch ale, compared to most kinds of beer, doesn't have a lot of hop flavor. In general, hops are added to beer because their bitterness balances out the sweetness of malt barley. Once a malt mash is distilled, though, presumably the "bite" of the higher alcohol content, along with the various esters, does the balancing. (Scotch ale is also higher in alcohol than a lot of other beers, which may compensate for the limited amount of hops used.) I have heard of whiskey made from hopped beer, but I've never tried it. One of these days, I'll make some Scotch ale and distill it, just to see for myself what would happen. I must admit the idea of hopped whiskey doesn't immediately appeal to me, but you never know.

Rye Whiskey

Historically, rye has been the primary ingredient in the production of schnapps and vodka in Germany. As the Germans emigrated to the United States, they brought their distilling skills with them. For many years, well into the early 20th century, rye whiskey was the most popular whiskey type on the eastern seaboard, especially in Pennsylvania and Maryland. Indeed, many consider rye whiskey to be the first indigenous American whiskey.

Legal Definitions of Various Whiskey Types (United States)

Bourbon: Must contain a minimum of 51% corn, be produced in the United States, be distilled at less than 160 proof (80% ABV) and be aged for a minimum of two years in new, charred oak barrels.

Tennessee Whiskey: Must contain a minimum of 51% corn, be distilled at less than 160 proof (80% ABV), be filtered through a bed of sugar-maple charcoal and be aged for a minimum of two years in new, charred oak barrels.

Rye Whiskey: Must contain a minimum of 51% rye grain, be distilled at less than 160 proof (80% ABV) and be aged for a minimum of two years in new, charred oak barrels.

Corn Whiskey: Must contain a minimum of 80% corn, be distilled at less than 160 proof (80% ABV) and be aged for a minimum of two years in new or used uncharred oak barrels.

Moonshine (white lightning or corn likker): Made from a mixture of corn and sugar, and aged in jugs or Mason jars.

Canadian Whiskey: Canadian whiskies are made primarily from corn or wheat, sometimes supplemented with rye, barley or barley malt. Nearly all Canadian whiskies are blends of different grain whiskies of varying ages. In Canada, there are no government requirements for the quantities and types of grains used for whiskey production. Canadian blended whiskies are, by definition, aged a minimum of three years, primarily in used oak barrels. The maximum aging time is ten years, although this is considered truly ancient by Canadian standards.

Rye whiskey production, after taking a major hit during Prohibition, had virtually disappeared from the eastern states by the 1980s. Today, the few distilleries still making rye whiskey use it mainly for blending, although some newer craft distilleries are exploring the possibilities of straight rye whiskey. The yield from rye tends to be lower than from malted barley and other grains, and not everyone cares for the relatively spicy character of rye whiskey.

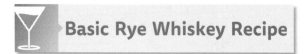

Basic Rye Whiskey Recipe

- 5 gallons (19 L) filtered or unchlorinated water
- 10 pounds (4.5 kg) cracked rye berries
- 2½ pounds (1.1 kg) malted rye
- 2½ pounds (1.1 kg) cracked malted barley
- 1 package whiskey yeast/enzyme combination
- 2 tablespoons plain yogurt or dried cheesemaking culture (optional)

Heat the water in a large stockpot to 71°C/160°F. Stir in the rye berries and malted rye, followed by the malted barley. Put the lid on the pot and hold the temperature at 66°–68°C/152°–155°F for 60 minutes. Test for starch conversion using the iodine test, and hold for up to another 60 minutes if necessary for full starch conversion.

Cool the mash to 33°C/92°F. Transfer the mash to an 8-gallon fermentation bucket. Add yeast and yogurt or cheese culture (if using). Ferment at room temperature for 2 or 3 days. Strain the liquid from the grains. Check and record the specific gravity of the wash.

Transfer the wash to your still and do a stripping run. The low wines should be about 30% ABV. Next do a spirit run, making the cut to hearts when the emerging distillate is down to 80% ABV. Switch to tails when the emerging distillate is down to 62%–65% ABV.

Rye whiskey is typically aged in heavily charred new oak barrels. Follow the guidelines in chapter 18, tossing in an extra handful of chips.

Tequila and
Sunchoke Spirit

I'm not actually much of a tequila drinker, but that's not for any particular reason. It just doesn't occur to me that often. Plus I like Irish whiskey, but that's another story.

I should say right now that, unless you are buying your ingredients wholesale, I doubt if it is cost-effective to make your own tequila. Not that economics is the only reason to make your own booze, of course. But good tequila (and you do want to make good tequila, right?) is made from 100% blue agave. I don't know about you, but here in the mountains of Washington State, I somehow doubt that blue agave would grow very well. If you live in southern California or the southwest, you may have easier access to agave.

Making tequila from agave syrup is relatively quick and easy, though, as it doesn't involve all that mashing that you do when making whiskey. It's more like making rum, since all you're doing is dissolving the syrup in water, fermenting and distilling it.

True tequila comes only from the Jalisco region of Mexico, where the blue agaves do love to grow. For ten years, they are cultivated before being harvested and cooked down into a sugary syrup that is then fermented and distilled. Some premium tequilas are aged, some for several years, but many are simply stored for a few months in stainless steel tanks before being bottled and sold.

Just to see what would happen, I shopped around and bought some organic free-trade blue agave syrup. I then had to experiment a bit with diluting the syrup in water, to come up with a wash with an OG of 1.070. This turned out to be 2 gallons of water for two 44-ounce bottles of agave syrup. I have seen recipes for tequila that call for adding sugar as well as the agave syrup. You can do this, and will probably save some money, but it won't be 100% agave spirit; you'll have something more like mezcal.

 Be careful what kind of agave syrup you buy for this experiment; some of them are highly processed. Look for raw agave syrup, preferably blue agave.

I was just distilling this batch of tequila about a week before turning in this manuscript, so I'll be curious to see how it turns out once it's aged (or "rested") a bit.

 ## Tequila (Agave Spirit)

- 2 bottles (44 oz. each) organic blue agave syrup
- 2 gallons (7.6 L) warm water, filtered or unchlorinated
- 1 package whiskey yeast/enzyme combination

Put 1 gallon of warm water in a fermenting bucket. Add the agave syrup and stir to dissolve. Stir in the second gallon of water. Check and record the specific gravity; it should be around 1.065 to 1.070. Make sure the temperature of the wash is 29°–33°C/85°–92°F and add the yeast. Put the lid and airlock in place and ferment.

Transfer the wash to your still and do a stripping run. Then do a spirit run on the low wines, distilling until the accumulated hearts are about 55% ABV.

I found that, in our relatively cool kitchen, this wash was a little slow to begin fermenting, but once it started, it fermented quite vigorously for nearly a week before slowing down. Just a reminder to not be too locked into the formulas in recipes; conditions vary a lot, so will your results. Remember to keep good records, and over time you will know what to do for the most consistent results.

Tequilas, at least the better ones, are usually "rested" for a minimum of two months before bottling, in stainless steel tanks. I definitely recommend resting your agave spirits for a month or two before drinking. You might set aside a small bottle for a longer period so you can compare results. Be sure to label the bottle with the date and the contents, and keep notes along the way. I know you're sick of me reminding you to keep records, but trust me, it pays off if you're aiming for great results over time.

Go to Your Stillhouse and Play!

I'm often asked what is the most interesting thing I've distilled so far. The first thing that comes to mind is the spirit I distilled from the local organic sunchokes (Jerusalem artichokes). Our friend Gabriel (chef of Sequim's Alder Wood Bistro) suggested it to me one day. I did some reading, and discovered that sunchokes are being used in the fuel-alcohol industry, as they have a considerable quantity of fermentable sugars. I wasn't able to find any actual recipes online for fermenting and distilling sunchokes, so I improvised some things, took guesses at others, and it pretty much went like that.

We bought 20 pounds of local organic sunchokes. I admit I had never bought such things before. Very interesting little tubers. They were small, knobby and firm. I guess I could have gone to the trouble of peeling them, but I didn't. I simply chopped them up into small pieces, dumped them in a big stainless steel stockpot, and covered them with what I hoped was an adequate amount of water. Simmered the things for hours before they were tender enough to be mashable.

One of many things that didn't occur to me at the time was to press the cooked tubers. What I did do was to scoop them out of the stockpot (this was after they had cooled down) and into a large straining bag inside a fermenting bucket. Just like those jelly bags your mother (OK, OK, your grandmother) used to use, only a lot bigger. I left it suspended like that overnight, and in the morning, I gave the bag an affectionate little squeeze, just in case those sunchokes wanted to give up a little bit more of those fermentable sugars.

This, by the way, was one of the first things I ever distilled. It was also just before it occurred to me to start keeping records of what I was up to. So unfortunately, I don't know for sure what kind of yeast I used for this, but a good guess would be one of those pre-packaged whiskey yeast/enzyme combinations.

I am quite sure, at this point, that the next time I make booze from sunchokes, my yields will be a lot higher; that's certainly true of other kinds of liquor I've distilled. I'm better at mashing, and better at making the cuts. I know now that I can add amylase enzymes to facilitate starch conversion during mashing. I would probably grind up something like sunchokes before cooking, to increase the surface area. Still, although I didn't get a huge quantity out of my first sunchoke distillation, I did get something that, to my inexperienced palate, has a smell and taste reminiscent of tequila.

Let this be a lesson to you, if you haven't already discovered it for yourself: You can probably distill some kind of booze from just about anything that has a reasonable amount of fermentable sugar (or starches that can be converted to fermentable sugar). I suggest sticking to tried-and-true recipes at first, until you get comfortable with all the various processes involved, before you go off to distill vodka from that three-year-old box of dried potato flakes or the bananas rapidly browning on the counter.

A Wide World of Possibilities

You've no doubt gotten the idea by this time that there is practically no limit to the things that can be produced in your stillhouse, once you have a little experience and the desire to continue improving your craft. Technically anything with starch or sugar in it can be converted into a distilled spirit. Who knows, you might be the one to discover the next best source of fuel ethanol. If what you aspire to is to learn to make one kind of distilled liquor really well, why then, do that. Distilling isn't the easiest thing to learn to do well, but in my opinion, it's certainly within reach of anyone willing to put some time and effort into the process.

Like so many things in life, you can learn only so much from books and blogs; most of what you will eventually learn will be by experience. And part of the fun of the experience is trying new things and seeing what works for you.

Don't Be So Immature:
Aging Small-batch Spirits

If you're someone whose motivation for making distilled spirits is to have something to drink fairly quickly, you can probably read the next section on diluting your spirits and then skip the rest of this chapter. I'm hoping, though, that you're someone who has been toiling to produce a super-premium whiskey or rum and wants to go the extra mile now by aging it. You've put this much work and time into it, after all; what's another few weeks or months in the grand scheme of things? You might forget that jar of whiskey resting on the shelf in the cupboard, only to discover it months later; imagine your surprise and delight to find that it rather closely resembles that pricey bourbon you used to buy.

Diluting Your Spirits

By the time you have finished your spirit run, the hearts that you've collected are likely to have an alcohol content of 65% ABV or more. At some point, you will want to dilute this potent spirit; drinking alcohol this strong is frankly dangerous. Also, flavor-positive spirits such as whiskey and brandy benefit from being diluted, in order to bring out the optimal flavors and aromas.

So how is this done? First, the water used for diluting spirits should ideally be free of calcium and magnesium; these elements are insoluble in water and may cause hazing. You can safely use tap water, although I suggest trying it first in a small amount of spirits to be sure it won't cause hazing or affect the flavor of the spirit. The water should obviously be flavor-neutral, so do not use chlorinated water.

That said, I have used our natural spring water (which is fairly high in calcium) to dilute several different kinds of spirits with good results. It's probably best to use filtered or distilled water, though, since that way you can be more sure of consistent results.

It's important to note that if you are going to be aging your spirits, especially on oak, you should not dilute the spirit to the desired drinking strength before it is aged. This is most often applicable to whiskey, which is optimally diluted to between 55% and 62% ABV before aging. It has been found that this alcohol concentration is ideal for extracting the desired compounds from the charred or toasted wood. Also, remember that some of the liquid will be lost to evaporation over time. Naturally this will be less of an issue when aging the relatively small amounts that we're discussing here, but it's still a good idea to get in the habit of doing things as professionally as possible. Once aging is complete, you can then check the alcohol content of your finished spirit and adjust the dilution accordingly.

First, check the temperature of the spirit and the water; ideally they will both be 20°C/68°F. Whatever the temperature, it is important that both the spirit and liquid be the same temperature. This can easily be accomplished by storing the spirit and water in the same room for several days.

Next, check the alcohol content of your spirit and record this number. Using the formula below, calculate how much water you should add to reach the desired alcohol content. Pour the water into the spirit, not the other way around. Mixing slowly will help prevent any haze from forming.

Calculating Dilution of Spirits

$$\frac{\text{Volume}}{\text{of hearts}} \times \frac{\text{\% ABV of hearts}}{\text{Desired \% ABV}} - \frac{\text{Volume}}{\text{of hearts}} = \frac{\text{Volume of}}{\text{water required}}$$

For example, say you have 2,000 ml of hearts at 95% ABV. You want to dilute it to 40% ABV.

$$2,000 \times \frac{95\%}{40\%} - 2,000 = 2,750 \text{ ml water required}$$

After dilution, this would produce 4.75 liters of spirit at 40% ABV.

 Mixing alcohol and water will result in a reduction of volume, due to contraction.

 If you are going to be filtering your spirit, try diluting it in stages, e.g., adding 10% of the water every 2 or 3 days. This causes larger particles to form which are more easily removed by filtration.

Aging: In Pursuit of the 18-year-old Malt Whiskey

There is a complicated calculation that deals with the ratio of surface area that a given amount of liquor is in contact with at any given time; this is supposed to enable you to decide how long to age your precious malt whiskey if you decide to put it in a 3-gallon barrel instead of a 15-gallon barrel. Since we're talking quite small quantities here, chances are very good that you won't even consider using a barrel to age your whiskey, even though there are barrels as small as 1 gallon available today.

I read somewhere that when you age liquor in small bottles, it ages much more quickly than in those 53-gallon barrels. In fact, the theory is that aging in a 1-gallon container for a month is equivalent

These American oak chips are easy to obtain and use for aging small batches of spirits.

to a *year* in a full-sized barrel. If true, said I to myself, it means that I could potentially have the equivalent of a 12-year-old malt whiskey in just a year!

I like to age my spirits in wide-mouth half-gallon Mason jars. That's plenty big for most of the batches I've made so far, with room in there for adding a few handfuls of charred or toasted oak chips. As soon as I have enough low wines accumulated, I'm going to do a malt-whiskey spirit run and set aside the hearts for 18 months. Our homestead

Toasting, Charring and Using Oak Chips

I know this is low-tech, but what can I say, I'm a homesteader and inclined to be thrifty and creative. I am used to roasting coffee beans in a cast iron pan on an outdoor propane burner, so I thought I would try toasting oak chips this way. Like coffee, it took some experimenting to find out how big a flame to use and for how long, but I've had some pretty good results.

There's not much to it. Put some oak chips in a cast iron pan; don't fill the pan much more than half full, though, as you will be shaking or stirring it constantly once it's heating up. Propane burners vary a lot in terms of BTU output, so try starting with a medium flame and go from there. Some oak chips can be quite small, and may burn easily, so take your time. I like to use a medium flame at first, then turn it down low as soon as I see a little smoke wafting up. Soon after the chips start heating, you will notice a distinctive vanilla scent; turn off the flame now if you just want a little toasted-oak flavor. I most often keep toasting until some of the chips are black around the edges and a fair amount of smoke is happening.

Tip: Do not be tempted to do this indoors; it does produce quantities of smoke.

Turn off the heat just before the chips are as dark as you want them to be; the pan is still quite hot and you don't want to over-char the chips. Let them cool before using; you don't want to toss chips into high-proof liquor when there might may not be as high up in the mountains as one of those Highland distilleries, but I'll bet we end up with something special. And a year and a half goes by pretty quickly.

Filtering

I read recently that the vast majority of commercially produced whiskey is filtered. This filtering can range from something akin to pouring through a sieve to a long slow process of filtering through

Whisky and other spirits get their color from charred oak chips.

be a spark hiding in the chips. If you're not going to use them right away, put the cooled chips in a clean jar and keep tightly covered.

How much chips should you use? I wish there was a definitive answer to this question. It depends a bit on what you're aging and how much spirit you have. I would say a general rule of thumb is to add about 2 to 3 handfuls to a quart of spirit, but then I have rather small hands. How about a cup or so instead of handfuls? You will see the color start to change not long after you drop in the chips. If it sits there for a week and it's not as dark as you'd like, try adding another handful or ½ cup more charred chips. Some of those really dark rums and whiskies have caramel coloring added, so don't expect

your liquor to get that dark from charred oak alone. As with so many parts of the distillation process, there is a lot of room for experimentation during the aging process.

Tip: You can also try using those little oak cubes called, for some reason, beans. Some people say beans are better than chips; I haven't tried using them myself, mainly because they are so much more expensive than oak chips. I wouldn't be surprised if there was a difference, since the thickness of the beans is something closer to the thickness of the staves in a barrel. On such a small scale, however, I'm a bit skeptical that it could really matter all that much. If you try the beans, do be careful when you're toasting or charring them.

a deep bed of charcoal (think Tennessee whiskey). In general, the purpose of filtering spirits is to purify the product by removing unwanted residual congeners and other undesirable flavor elements. Presumably it also helps ensure some degree of consistency between batches.

In the case of commercial vodka, which in the United States is legally defined as a neutral spirit, this filtering is very important. With whiskey and other flavor-positive spirits such as brandy, there is a risk that some desirable elements may be removed along with the undesirable ones. On a small or non-commercial scale, I suggest you filter your vodka but not other spirits.

Activated carbon and activated charcoal are technically the same thing, but neither is the same thing as charcoal. Be sure to use only food-grade activated carbon for filtering your spirits.

Activated carbon is available in several forms: powdered, pelletized or granular. Pelletized carbon is often used to filter water where the water is circulated (e.g. in an aquarium). The granular type is best for filtering spirits as its surface area is large and there is good access to the pores that facilitate filtration.

Most of the congener molecules targeted by filtration are between 2 and 10 nanometers in size. The pores in carbon are created during the activation process, and are of different sizes: Macro (>25 nm), meso (1 to 25 nm) and micro (<1 nm).

The most common materials used for making activated carbon for alcohol filtration are peat, stone coal and coconut shells. The grain size (also called mesh size) commonly used in spirits filtration are 20 × 40 (0.4–0.85 mm) and 14 × 40 (0.4–1.4 mm); 20 × 40 is a good middle-ground size that is easy to find, has good filtration speed, and low risk of clogging during filtration.

Filtration works by trapping molecules within the carbon pores. Thus, liquid must be forced through the carbon, not just channeled around the grains. A common mistake is throwing the activated carbon into a bucket of liquor; it will simply settle to the bottom of the bucket, and very little of the spirit will actually enter the carbon pores.

The Process

So, you have some premium vodka that you're simply dying to try, but you want to filter it first. I recommend storing it for a week or two before filtering, at a cold temperature: ideally −5°–0°C/23°–32°F. Even if you can't store it that cold, do remember that it is best to filter it at the same temperature it was stored at.

Ideally you will have a long filter bed, to maximize the contact between liquid and carbon. I use a nifty setup called the Carbon Snake (see Resources). This is a simple tube, about 30 inches long, that connects to the spigot of a fermenting bucket containing the spirit to be filtered. The activated carbon is poured into the tube, then primed by adding warm water to the tube. The spigot is then opened, and the spirit begins to flow through the carbon bed. A large jar or bottle at the other end of the tube collects the filtered spirit.

For best results, dilute your spirit to no more than 55% ABV before filtering. Higher-proof spirits have lower density, which causes it to tend to flow around the carbon grains. On the other hand, it isn't efficient to dilute it much below 55% ABV; this just means you have more liquid to filter so it takes longer. In addition, the filtration process changes the proof slightly, so it makes sense to filter it first, then dilute to the desired drinking strength. (**Note:** The Carbon Snake recommends diluting to no more than 50% ABV before filtering.)

The instructions with the Carbon Snake say that the slower the flow, the purer the finished spirit. The first time I used it, I was filtering only about two liters of vodka. I'm not kidding, it took about eight hours to filter that amount. But that is some tasty vodka!

Here is a nifty trick to eliminate the need to filter your spirits, if you are filtering to prevent hazing. Add water to the spirit until the ABV is 55%. Add remaining water in a slow, gentle drip; this will ensure virtually no hazing at least down to 43% ABV. No aroma substances will be lost, since no filtering is necessary. Recheck the ABV and adjust if needed.

Diluting spirits to less than 45% ABV often results in hazing because some substances (fusel oils, esters, terpene, calcium and magnesium) are only soluble at higher alcohol concentrations and will precipitate. It's important to note that these substances cannot be removed by filtration.

Bottling

Brandy and schnapps expand in heat and contract in cold. An ideal temperature for both measuring alcohol content and determining the quantity to go into each bottle is 20°C/68°F.

After drinking strength is set, store your spirits for at least several weeks in a warm dark place. Don't let it get too warm, though; if the bottles are in a place where they may get hot, bottle breakage may occur as the ethanol expands.

Brandy, Liqueurs and Other Excuses to Spend More Time in the Stillhouse

On a European trip in 2002, David and I spent a few days in northern France. While staying in Rouen, we rented a car and drove north and west to visit Omaha Beach, one of the D-Day landing beaches of World War II. An uncle of mine, a captain in the 29th Infantry Division, was killed six days after D-Day and is buried at the American cemetery on the bluff above the beach.

It was my second visit to this cemetery, the first for David. After spending a few emotional hours there, we headed back toward Rouen. On the way, we drove through miles of the beautiful rolling hills and apple orchards of Normandy. We stopped at a farm advertising cider, hoping to sample and perhaps buy some local specialties. At the time, my French was just good enough to carry on a conversation without too much trouble. We were the only visitors, and the lovely Frenchwoman in the farm store was very friendly. She seemed quite charmed to discover that we actually knew about Calvados, the world-famous apple brandy of Normandy. Soon she had lined up several glasses on the counter, proceeding to pour samples of ciders and brandies of ever-increasing age and alcoholic potency, and she urged us to try them all.

Not wishing to appear ungrateful, we obliged, starting with a delightful sweet cider of 2% alcohol. When we eventually swam our way to the final sample, Madame, with a conspiratorial smile (she may also have winked), announced it as being Calvados. I had never tasted Calvados before. I tell you, it was a revelation. After the brief, fiery, first tiny sip, the spirit seemed to linger in my mouth for hours, revealing layers of flavor I can't even begin to describe accurately.

And after all that, Madame wouldn't let us pay for a thing! She seemed simply pleased to share the fruits of the farm's labors with visitors who truly appreciated the craftsmanship of their work.

I suppose that's what initially planted a seed in the back of my mind. I remember thinking how wonderful it would be to learn to make cider like that, much less a magical elixir like apple brandy. By the time we moved to the farm in 2006, I was looking at all those old apple trees (originally planted by David's grandmother) with different ideas.

Last fall, after several years of cider-making experience, I finally started working on my first batch of what I optimistically hoped would become apple brandy. As usual, I bought a book on the subject of brandy (see Books in Appendix A), and studied until I felt confident enough to try.

Making Fruit Brandy

Brandies are distilled from wine or fermented fruit or grape mashes. Whole books have been written on the subject of distilling brandy, but I will attempt a fairly concise overview of the process here. While there are some similarities in the fermentation and distilling processes compared to making other kinds of liquor, brandy production also has unique requirements.

Commercially and historically, brandy has been produced using a special kind of still, the alembic still. Its unique design facilitates the retention of desirable flavor elements in the particular fruit being distilled. It is basically a specialized pot still, and many different sizes and types are available today. As you know, my main still is a small column still, capable of behaving like a pot still. I thought it would be worth trying to make brandy.

The first batch of brandy I distilled was made from a finished white wine I had started several years earlier. Originally this wine, a French chardonnay, was destined to be made into champagne. Long story short, it didn't turn out as I had hoped, so I never did re-ferment it for champagne. It was still sealed with an airlock in a carboy, though, so at least it hadn't turned to vinegar in the meantime.

I was planning to start making orange liqueur (see recipe on page 149) for David. His favorite thing in the morning is to make hot cocoa, to which he adds a shot of dark rum and half a shot of orange liqueur. (Delicious, but I don't like sugar or alcohol in the mornings; do try it if you're so inclined!) He was bemoaning the fact that most commercial orange brandies are vodka-based, while he preferred the ones that are brandy-based (like Cointreau).

So I had a brainwave. Why not put that unloved chardonnay to good use and distill it into brandy? I had about five gallons of the stuff. I thought it was worth a try, anyway. I followed my usual procedure of doing a stripping run first, ending up with about two liters of low wines. I decided that, for that small amount, it would be more efficient to do the spirit run in the small essential-oil distiller.

It worked just fine, although I had to do it in batches. My small distiller has a capacity of two liters; it technically could hold all my low wines, but at 45% ABV, I knew better than to fill that boiling pot that full. As you may remember, ethanol expands when it is heated, and I didn't want to risk it boiling over and possibly starting a fire. So I split the low wines into two batches. It really didn't take much more time than doing it in one batch, since one liter comes to a boil quite quickly in a small boiling pot.

The brandy turned out great. I put the finished raw spirit in a glass jar, diluted it to 45% ABV and added a couple of handfuls of toasted and charred oak chips. In about a month, it had smoothed out noticeably and had a nice golden color to it. It wasn't your basic hundred-year-old Napoleon brandy, but it did make a fantastic orange liqueur.

Procedure

You can use many different kinds of fruits, of course, including some interesting ones like quince and juniper berries. We have a lot of quince and apple trees here, but our quinces haven't had much fruit lately, probably due to inadequate pollination. However, the apple trees produced quite a nice crop last fall, so we crushed and pressed about 150 pounds to be fermented and distilled into apple brandy.

Use only fully ripe, clean, healthy fruit for making brandy. Discard any fruits that are visibly rotten, wrinkled, damaged or green. Always wash the fruit, even if it appears clean. Washing will minimize the amount of mildew, vinegar bacteria and undesirable yeasts in the fruit.

Pomace left over from pressing crushed apples. Chickens and turkeys love it!

Crushing and Pressing Fruit

After we picked our apples, we stored them in boxes in a cold room for several weeks before pressing. This facilitates crushing and pressing by breaking down the cell walls of the fruit; it also results in an increased yield of juice. We have a nice hand-crank apple crusher and a good-sized press, which are useful for large quantities of fruit. For smaller amounts, you might try coarsely chopping the fruit in a food processor (be careful not to let the fruit heat up).

When mashing stone fruits, stones must remain whole. The stones contain prussic acid, so be very careful.

Enzyme Treatment of Fruit Mash

Enzymes are active substances that affect chemical processes without being consumed. Usually a specific enzyme causes one specific reaction, although complicated metabolic processes require more than one enzyme. For example, alcoholic fermentation needs twelve different enzymes.

Pectic enzyme makes fruit mashes more liquid by breaking down pectin in the fruit. Pectic enzyme is optimally effective at 40°–50°C/104°–122°F, although satisfactory results can occur at temperatures as low as 18°–20°C/64°–68°F. Once the temperature drops below 10°C/50°F, enzyme activity virtually ceases. Good distribution of the enzymes in the mash is critical for good results; this is best achieved by thinning the enzyme with a little water or fruit juice, then adding the enzyme mixture to the fruit during the milling or crushing process.

Concentrated pectic enzyme is available in various quantities at homebrew supply shops. Different fruits naturally have varying amounts of pectin, so follow the directions on the package to determine the quantity to be used.

Advantages of enzyme treatment, especially with pectin-rich pome fruits, include:

- Rapid liquefaction of mash
- Faster, more complete fermentation
- Less formation of foam during fermentation
- Better heat transmission during distillation (due to a thinner mash consistency)
- Easier stirring of mash during fermentation

Using enzymes with stone fruits helps stones separate from the fruit more easily, and is especially recommended when mashing firm-fleshed fruits.

NOTE: At best, using enzymes results in minimal increase in alcohol yield. This is most likely due to the enzyme treatment enabling easier mashing and more complete fermentation. Enzyme treatment produces no noticeable effect on the flavor of the finished brandy.

Pectic enzyme will be effective for up to a year when kept refrigerated. At room temperature, its effectiveness decreases by 1% to 2% per month, so try to buy only as much as you need for one season.

pH of Known Liquids

Liquid	pH
Hydrochloric acid	0 (extremely acidic)
Sulfuric acid	1.2
Tartaric acid	2.2
Vinegar	3.1
Wine, fruit mashes	3.0–3.8
Apple mash, fermented	3.5–4.2 (with table fruit)
Apple mash, fermented	3.0–3.5 (with must fruit)
Pear mash, fermented	3.7–4.0 (with table fruit)
Pear mash, fermented	3.4–3.8 (with must fruit)
Beer	4.0–5.0
Pure water	7 (neutral)
Sea water	8.3
Soda solution (0.5%)	11.3
Lime water, saturated	12.3
Caustic soda	14.0 (extremely alkaline)

The Importance of Being Acidic

Minimum acid levels are necessary for good fermentation of fruit mashes. Addition of acid is recommended for acid-poor fruits such as Golden Delicious apples, raspberries, elderberries, apricots, peaches, etc. The optimum pH of fruit mash should be between 2.5 and 4.5 (ideal is 3.0 to 3.2) for proper enzyme and yeast activity.

Acid can be added in one of two ways. One, add yeast and enzyme first, and mix two or three times over several hours. Next, check the pH and add acid as directed on the package. Two, check pH and acidify first, mix well, then add yeast and enzyme. If using this second method, aim for a pH of 3.0 to 3.2.

If fruit is not fully ripened when mashed, starches may still be present. If you're not sure, use the iodine test (see chapter 8) to check for starch. Add amylase enzyme according to package directions if needed for starch conversion.

Fermentation

As you know by now, there are many different strains of commercially available yeast for making all kinds of fermented and distilled beverages. Fruit brandies are no exception to this rule. Honestly, I don't have enough experience with making brandy to be able to recommend one type over another. I suggest you get a good book on the subject (see Books in Appendix A). If at all possible, talk to people with experience making brandy, maybe a local distillery, and ask them for recommendations.

When I made my first batch of apple brandy, I used (not knowing any better) a liquid Wyeast brand cider yeast from the local homebrew shop. It did ferment the apple juice out fairly quickly, although the next time, I will put the fermenting bucket in a warmer spot.

A good strong fermentation is necessary for producing aroma and flavor substances from the yeast. Optimal fermentation also discourages formation of undesirable substances that form unpleasant flavors and aromas.

Ideal fermentation temperature is 18°–20°C/64°–68°F. Yeast ceases fermentation at 40°C/104°F, and dies at 60°C/140°F. Especially in small batches, it's important to keep the fermentation temperature

My first batch of ginger liqueur; fresh ginger makes all the difference.

Brandy-based orange liqueur.

at least 18°C/64°F. For best results, make sure the fruit used is at least 18°C/64°F when it is mashed.

Before distilling brandy, be sure to clean your still, especially if it's been a while since it has been used. Here is the cleaning procedure often used in commercial brandy distilleries.

1. Flush the still with hot water (70°C/158°F is ideal) for 2 minutes.
2. Flush with caustic soda solution (or dishwashing detergent solution) at 60°C/140°F for 10 to 15 minutes.
3. Flush with warm water for about 5 minutes.
4. Flush with 2% citric acid solution (30°C/86°F) for 10 minutes.
5. Flush with warm or cold water for about 2 minutes.

It's up to you how particular you want to be about cleaning your still. My feeling is that, considering how relatively small my still is, the flushing times above are probably more than is necessary. I like to flush with hot water, then with the citric acid solution, then with warm water. Since the condenser tube on my still is open at the top, I simply close the needle valve and pour the hot water, etc., into the condenser tube. It runs through the still head and column into the boiling pot below (make sure the pot is empty first!).

Distillation

Since aroma is such a critical element in fruit brandies, it is particularly important to begin distillation when fermentation is winding down or just barely done. Fruits with more delicate aromas should definitely be distilled before fermentation is actually completed.

As with distilling other quality spirits, I highly recommend that you do a stripping run on your brandy first, then a spirit run. After the stripping run, be sure to record the quantity and ABV of your low wines. This will help you estimate the quantity of hearts you will collect during the spirit run; the hearts should be equivalent to about 30% of the total quantity of low wines.

During the spirit run, remember to run the still fairly slowly to facilitate separation of the hearts from the heads and tails. Unlike most other spirits, you should begin to collect brandy hearts when the ABV of the emerging distillate has dropped to about 70%. Continue collecting hearts until the distillate has dropped to about 55% ABV; with some fruits, you can collect hearts down closer to 45% ABV. Once the ABV is down to 55%, try to taste the distillate frequently so you can determine when the tails are showing up.

Once you have definitely switched to tails, the distillation can be sped up a bit if desired. The tails will account for about 20% to 25% of the volume of low wines.

Special Distillation Notes

For aromatic fruits such as Williams Christ pears, the heads can contain large quantities of aromatic substances. After the spirit run, you can mix the heads and tails together and redistill them, heating slowly. Collect heads and hearts as before, but end the hearts phase between 50% and 60% ABV. The hearts from this after-run can be blended with the hearts from the first spirit run, or even used for a special brandy distillation, such as juniper berry brandy.

Methanol in Brandy

Enzymes in fruit convert pectin to methanol, which is poisonous. Methanol boils at 64.6°C/148.28°F. There is no good way to completely remove methanol, so small amounts will always be present in the heads, hearts and tails.

Maximum allowable methanol in fruit brandies: 2.2 pounds (1,000 g) per 26.4 gallons (100 L) alcohol. Exceptions: 2.6 pounds (1,200 g) allowed in brandies of apple, pear (except Williams Christ pears), damsons, plums, mirabelles, raspberries and blackberries; 3.0 pounds.(1,350 g) allowed in brandies of Williams Christ pears, quinces, black elder, currants, rowan berry and juniper berry.

Aging and Storing Brandy

Before diluting brandy hearts, it's best to store the raw brandy for 6 to 8 weeks in a dark place, at 15°–20°C/59°–68°F. Some exposure to oxygen is needed at this stage, so don't fill containers too full, and make sure lids are somewhat loose. If the storage area is cooler than 15°C/59°F, aging takes longer; temperatures warmer than 20°C/68°F may result in loss of alcohol through evaporation. Some brandies are aged in oak, but if you opt to try this, check the brandy frequently and remove it from the oak before too much wood flavor develops. Brandy is best stored in containers of glass, glazed earthenware or stainless steel.

Infused Liqueurs

Infusion is an easy method of making a wide variety of liqueurs. Many of the world's most famous liqueurs are made using this method. Like Angostura bitters, which is also an infusion, there are often closely guarded formulas behind liqueurs, involving an amazing array of herbs and spices. In spite of the secrecy, though, liqueurs can be easily made in your home distillery. Don't be intimidated by long lists of ingredients; if you've been making bitters or gin using these actual "botanicals" rather than flavorings, you already have a good start.

Infusions are made by soaking, or infusing, various ingredients in a base liquor, often vodka. Infusion times can be anywhere from a couple of days to many weeks. Generally the herbs and spices are infused, then strained out of the liquid. By definition, liqueurs are sweetened; usually this is done after the botanicals have been infused. Liqueurs may be sweetened with sugar, sugar syrup, honey or even agave syrup. One of the reasons I like making my own liqueurs is I have some control over how sweet I make them. David likes to add a little orange liqueur to his hot-cocoa-and-rum, and we experimented for quite a while adding simple syrup to the infusion, before coming up with just the right amount of sweetness to suit his taste.

Here are some recipes for popular liqueurs to get you started. I mentioned that David prefers orange liqueur with a brandy base rather than vodka; whichever base liquor you use for your infusions, choose something of good quality. You will notice the difference, I promise.

 ## David's Orange Liqueur

- About 32 ounces (1 L) brandy (homemade or at least not the cheapest stuff out there)
- 2 pounds (0.9 kg) organic mandarin oranges
- ½ cup (125 ml) dried organic sweet orange peel (purchased or homemade; see page 108)
- Simple syrup (see recipe below)

Note: I highly recommend using organic citrus fruits any time you're using the peel; non-organic fruits may have pesticide residues that you don't want in your infusions, so it's easier to avoid these by choosing organic.

Have two clean 1-quart wide-mouth Mason jars ready. Peel the mandarin oranges and cut the peels into fairly small pieces; this increases the surface area of the peel that will be exposed to the brandy. Divide the peel between the two jars. Add half of the dried orange peel to each jar. Add brandy to each jar to within about an inch of the top. Put lids on. Let the jars sit at room temperature, away from the sun, for at least 2 days; I have let it go up to a week with good results. Shake the jars gently at least once a day. After the first 2 days, begin smelling the infusion every day and stop infusing when the aroma is agreeable to you.

Strain the fruit out of the brandy. You should have around 25 to 28 ounces (750 to 875 ml) of liquid. Add simple syrup to taste and bottle. As a guideline, we used 1 teaspoon (5 ml) simple syrup for each fluid ounce of liqueur; add a little at a time and taste until the sweetness suits you, and be sure to make a note of how much simple syrup you used! I suspect you will like this liqueur so much that you will be making it again.

The liqueur is ready to use, but I recommend letting it sit in a cool dark place for at least a month.

Simple Syrup

Bring equal quantities of sugar and water to a boil in a covered saucepan. Let cool. Tastes in sweetness vary, so I can't tell you exactly how much to make for this liqueur recipe. Start with 1 cup (250 ml) of sugar and 1 cup (250 ml) of water. Store any extra in the fridge and use promptly.

David's Hot Cocoa and Rum

Make a nice big mug of hot cocoa; David likes his favorite 16-ounce mug for this. You can use your favorite hot cocoa mix, although David prefers the kind made by adding hot water instead of milk. Leave enough room in the mug for 1 shot of dark rum (definitely not light rum for this) and ½ shot of orange liqueur.

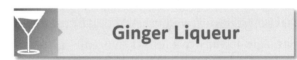

Ginger Liqueur

- 2 ounces (60 g) fresh ginger root, peeled
- 1 vanilla bean
- 1 cup (250 g) sugar (or ¾ cup (175 ml) honey)
- 1½ cups (375 ml) water
- Zest of 1 organic orange or ¼ cup (60 ml) dried organic orange peel
- 1½ cups (375 ml) brandy

Again, I recommend using brandy as the base for this delicious liqueur. Slice the ginger thinly. Split the vanilla bean lengthwise.

In a saucepan, bring the ginger, vanilla bean, sugar and water to a boil. Lower heat and simmer for 20 minutes. Remove from heat and let cool.

Pour the syrup into a jar (don't strain it), add the orange zest or peel and the brandy. Seal, give it a shake, and let it steep for a day; remove the vanilla bean and let it steep at least one more day. I let mine steep for 5 days total with good results, but then I like a lot of ginger flavor.

Strain into a bottle. Let it sit for at least 2 weeks (if you can stand it) before using.

Upper Dungeness Bourbon Smash for Two (It's Too Good Not to Share)

- 2 ounces (60 ml) ginger liqueur
- 2 ounces (60 ml) bourbon
- ½ organic lemon

Put the ginger liqueur and lemon in a cocktail shaker or mixing glass. Muddle well with muddler or a long wooden spoon. Add about one cup of cracked ice and the bourbon. Stir well until the glass is frosty. Pour into cocktail glass or wine glass; do not strain. Garnish with a lemon slice.

Purists will insist a smash isn't a smash without mint, so go ahead and garnish with fresh mint if you like.

Coffee Liqueur

- 1 recipe cold-brewed coffee (see below)
- ½ cup (125 ml) water
- ½ cup (125 ml) dark brown sugar (packed)
- 1 cup (250 ml) dark rum
- ½ vanilla bean

First make the cold-brewed coffee. Bring the water and brown sugar to a boil on high heat; lower heat to a simmer, stirring to dissolve the sugar. Remove from the heat and let cool to room temperature, about 30 minutes.

Add the cooled syrup and rum to the jar with the coffee. Using a knife, split the vanilla bean in half lengthwise and scrape out the seeds, add both the seeds and pod to the coffee mixture and stir to combine. Put the lid back on the jar and let it sit at room temperature in a cool, dark place for at least 2 weeks, shaking once a day. Remove vanilla bean.

Note: David doesn't like anything that tastes like coffee, so at least I know he's not going to raid my stash in the middle of the night. I love this liqueur for just sipping, poured over a really good vanilla ice cream or...you get the idea. I haven't actually tried dunking a doughnut in coffee liqueur yet (don't know what's wrong with me), but I think it's worth trying, don't you?

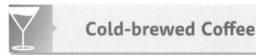

Cold-brewed Coffee

- ¾ cup (175 ml) coarsely ground coffee
- 1¾ cups (425 ml) water

Put the coffee in a 1-quart Mason jar, add the water and stir to combine. Put the lid on the jar and let steep at room temperature for at least 12 hours or up to 1 day.

Put a regular coffee filter inside a fine-mesh strainer and arrange over a medium bowl; I like to use my smaller strainer set on one of those canning funnels. Slowly pour the coffee into the filter until all of the liquid has passed through the strainer; take your time and don't force it through. Pour as much of the liquid in as you can before any of the coffee grounds get in the strainer. Put the grounds in the compost bucket along with whatever solids are in the strainer. Transfer the coffee to a 1-quart container and set it aside.

Handmade Bitters

What the heck are bitters? And why should you even think about making your own? If you're a connoisseur of classic cocktails, you're no doubt aware that, in the last few years, bitters are showing up all over the cocktail scene. Bartenders and mixologists are more and more frequently concocting their own unique bitters, often inspired by local ingredients.

Prior to Prohibition, bitters were considered an essential ingredient in many popular cocktails; often just a drop or two was the difference between an average drink and something more like ambrosia. But what exactly are bitters, and why are they so important to so many cocktails?

Long before bitters gained fame as an essential cocktail ingredient, they were concocted and consumed under many different names as patent medicines. Prior to the introduction of pharmaceuticals around the mid-1800s, homemakers and doctors relied heavily on herbal-based remedies. At that time, there were literally hundreds of these patent medicines on the market, like Dr. Hostetter's Stomach Bitters. Usually these remedies had an alcohol base; this was because many herbs were quite perishable as well as available only seasonally, and the alcohol served the practical purpose of preserving the fragile herbs.

To be clear, many bitters formulas were developed by physicians, and were marketed as *digestifs*, or stomach settlers. Other formulas were reputed (or at least claimed) to be effective cures for overindulgence (read: hangovers), headaches, stomach cramps and other digestive complaints. Formulas contained combinations of spices, herbs, tree bark, seeds, citrus fruit peels and other "botanicals," all infused in some sort of high-proof alcoholic spirit. Some of the best-known herbal liqueurs like Sambuca and Chartreuse have recipes based on bitters formulas.

The famous Angostura bitters, partly famous for its fanatically guarded secret formula, was developed by a German doctor, Johann Siegert. When he arrived in Venezuela in 1820, he was appointed surgeon general to Simon Bolivar's army, which was based in the town of Angostura. His knowledge of herbal remedies led him to create various tonics to help stimulate the soldiers' appetites and treat digestive complaints. His bitters later gained a loyal following among sailors in the Caribbean, who claimed it was a cure for seasickness.

Even during Prohibition, "new" bitters appeared on the market, labeled as somewhat tongue-in-cheek medicines, although they were often simply a clever legal way of serving a thirsty clientele. Indeed, even today bitters are considered a food additive and not a beverage, so they can be found on grocery store shelves and bought by anyone.

You might be wondering why bitters are so important in so many cocktail recipes. Besides adding a subtle layer of additional flavor, bitters, properly used, help balance out the sweetness of other ingredients, such as simple syrup or liqueur. David will absolutely, positively never make a Cuba Libre (see recipe on page 167) without using bitters; all that Coca-Cola would be too sweet even for his taste. (We almost never drink soda other than using it as a mixer.)

My first attempt at home-made orange bitters. The color is completely natural, derived from fresh and dried orange peel.

Making Your Own Bitters

When I picked up a copy of Brad Parsons' book *Bitters* (see Books in Appendix A), I had only just started to collect some of the herbs and spices I wanted for making gin. I didn't know I would want to make bitters when I bought the book; I was mostly just interested in learning more about them and how to use them. That changed when I realized I already had some of the ingredients in my growing apothecary of gin botanicals. That's probably why I went for the orange bitters first; I only had to buy a few additional ingredients like, well, oranges.

A word of caution: This can become an absorbing, not to say addictive, hobby. Once you collect enough basic ingredients to make a couple kinds of bitters, and you've had a chance to try your handmade concoctions, I'll bet you'll want to start coming up with your own recipes. There are plenty of recipes for all kinds of bitters on the Internet. I recommend you pick up a copy of *Bitters* and start with those recipes, both for bitters and the cocktails to use them in. There are even ideas for using bitters in other ways in the kitchen, such as in salad dressings and glazes for meat.

Here is a recipe for orange bitters, which is based on the recipe in *Bitters*. I was amazed at the beautiful orange color it developed, all from the fresh peel. Look for the gentian root (don't leave it out; it's an important bittering ingredient) at your local natural foods store, or order from Starwest Botanicals (see Resources).

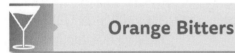

Orange Bitters

- Zest of 3 organic oranges, cut into thin strips
- ¼ cup (60 ml) dried organic orange peel
- 4 whole cloves
- 8 green cardamom pods, cracked
- ¼ teaspoon (1 ml) coriander seeds
- ½ teaspoon (2 ml) dried gentian root
- ¼ teaspoon (1 ml) whole allspice
- 2 cups (0.5 L) high-proof vodka (don't skimp on cheap brands here)
- 1 cup (250 ml) water
- 2 tablespoons (30 ml) Rich Syrup (recipe below)

Put the orange zest, dried orange peel, spices and gentian root into a 1-quart Mason jar. Add the vodka, adding a bit more if needed to completely cover the ingredients. Put on the lid and store at room temperature for 2 weeks. Shake the jar gently once a day.

Strain the liquid, using cheesecloth or a coffee filter, into a clean 1-quart Mason jar. Repeat straining until all sediment is removed. Squeeze the cheesecloth to force through as much liquid as possible. Transfer the solids to a small saucepan. Cover the jar and set aside.

Pour the water over the solids in the saucepan and bring to a boil on medium heat. Cover the pan, reduce the heat to low and simmer for 10 minutes. Remove from heat and let cool completely.

Add the liquid and solids in the saucepan to another 1-quart Mason jar. Cover and store at room temperature for a week, shaking the jar every day. Strain the solids out, using cheesecloth, and discard the solids. Add the liquid to the jar with the original vodka mixture. Add the rich syrup, stir to mix well, then put the lid on and shake to blend and dissolve the syrup.

Store the jar at room temperature for 3 days. Then skim off anything that floats to the surface and strain it once more through cheesecloth. Use a funnel to bottle it, and you're done! These bitters have the best flavor if used within a year, although they will last almost indefinitely.

Rich Syrup

Combine ½ cup (125 ml) sugar and ¼ cup (60 ml) water in a small saucepan. Bring to a boil, stir to dissolve sugar and remove from heat. Let cool before using.

For some classic cocktails using your handmade bitters, turn to chapter 22.

Making Your Own Mixers

This might seem a bit over-the-top to some people. I mean, why in the world would you bother making your own mixers? When I first started making orange liqueur in late 2014, I wasn't even thinking of it as a mixer; it was actually a Christmas present for David. Now we're using it in Cosmopolitans, Margaritas, and any cocktail that calls for Triple Sec, Cointreau or Grand Marnier.

For us, making some of our own mixers means being able to control both ingredients and sweetness. David tends to like more sweetness in certain drinks than I do, so I really appreciate being able to enjoy the same drinks with less sugar in them.

Tonic Water

For a long time, tonic water was the one thing we bought, even though we knew it had high-fructose corn syrup (HFCS) in it. We'd been trying hard to eliminate HFCS from our diet, and decided that we were just going to live with it in this case. The Gin & Tonic was usually a summertime drink for us, so what the heck. I don't remember what prompted me to look into the possibility of making our own tonic water, as opposed to looking for some other more hip commercial brand. But I did, and here we are.

I found this recipe on Jeffrey Morgenthaler's website. This popular Portland bartender, who is clearly elevating his mixology skills to a truly artistic level, says: "My problem with homemade tonic water has always been a flavor profile that was too esoteric for the general audience. This recipe takes some of the positive qualities people have come to understand from commercial tonic water and updated them with fresh ingredients." With Jeff's permission, I include here his own recipe.

Homemade Tonic Water

Homemade syrups for making tonic water (left) and ginger ale.

- 4 cups (1 L) water
- 1 cup (250 ml) chopped lemongrass (roughly one large stalk)
- ¼ cup (60 ml) powdered cinchona bark
- zest and juice of 1 orange
- zest and juice of 1 lemon
- zest and juice of 1 lime
- 1 teaspoon (5 ml) whole allspice berries
- ¼ cup (60 ml) citric acid
- ¼ tsp (1 ml) kosher salt

Combine ingredients in a medium saucepan and bring to a boil over high heat. Once mixture starts to boil, reduce heat to low, cover and simmer for 20 minutes. Remove from heat and strain out solids

I've had very good results simply letting the mixture stand undisturbed for at least a few days, and up to a week. This works especially well in the refrigerator. The solids settle to the bottom, and you can either rack the clear liquid off or carefully pour it into another clean jar. It takes a bit longer this way, but I think it's worth it.

using a strainer or chinois. You'll need to fine-strain the mixture, as it still contains quite a bit of the cinchona bark. You can use a coffee filter and wait for an hour or more, or do as I do and run the whole mixture through a French coffee press.

Once you're satisfied with the clarity of your mix, heat it back up on the stovetop or in the microwave, and then add ¾ cup of *agave syrup* to each cup of your hot mix. Stir until combined, and store in the attractive bottle of your choice.

You now have a syrup that you can carbonate with seltzer water; I use my iSi soda siphon for some nicely textured bubbles. To assemble a Gin & Tonic, combine ¾ ounce of syrup, 1½ ounces of gin and 2 ounces of soda water over ice.

Cinchona Bark

The bark of the cinchona tree, indigenous to Peru and Bolivia, is the natural source of quinine. Jeff advises:

> Try a few different suppliers for powdered cinchona bark to see which you like best. Tenzing Momo has great products as a rule, but their cinchona can often be floral, which may or may not work for you. You can also find cinchona from bulk herbal medicine retailers and other specialty herb shops. I find the yellow variety to be milder than the red, so adding too many other flavors to the mix can overpower the quinine. Adjust your recipes accordingly.

More tips from Jeff:

> Once you've mastered your own tonic recipe, you can begin to experiment with different spices and fruit flavors to pair with specific gins. For instance, I've found that beefing up the orange peel results in a tonic that pairs nicely with Hendrick's, but try playing off the coriander or cardamom in other gins and see what happens.

Canyon Creek Farms Ginger Syrup

I have been asked often for this ginger syrup recipe. It was another of those things that we came up with in our efforts to avoid products with HFCS. A drink we both like is Canadian whiskey and ginger ale (see recipe page 169), and we had been buying Canada Dry ginger ale for a mixer. After trying two or three different "natural" ginger ales, we got a bit frustrated; some actually had HFCS, others had a ginger taste that was just too hot to work well as a mixer.

Prepare 6 1-quart canning jars and lids. (Recipe yields about 6 quarts.) I usually keep the canning jars hot by leaving them full of very hot water in the sink. Have 6 rings ready. Bring your canning jar lids to a boil in a small saucepan of hot water. As soon as the water boils, turn off heat and keep covered until ready to use.

 You can, of course, make ginger syrup without canning. You will need to refrigerate it, though, as it may develop mold or begin to ferment if left out at room temperature. (See page 162 for quantities of ingredients for a 1-quart batch.)

In a stainless steel or enamel stockpot, combine:
- 9 cups (2.04 kg) sugar (I use organic white sugar; brown sugar gives a different flavor)
- 18 cups (4.3 L) water, preferably unchlorinated or filtered
- 6 ounces (180 g) fresh organic ginger, thinly sliced (peeled or unpeeled, as you prefer)

Cover and bring to a boil over medium-high heat, stirring to dissolve sugar. Once the syrup comes to a rolling boil, turn off heat. Leave the lid on and let steep for at least 10 minutes. While the syrup is heating, thinly peel and juice:

- 3 organic lemons (since you're using the peel, you really want to use organic lemons for this)

Divide the lemon peel pieces into 6 even piles. Remove ginger pieces from syrup with a slotted spoon or small sieve. Strain the seeds from the lemon juice and add juice to the hot syrup.

Taking the jars one at a time, empty out the water and put one pile of the lemon peel in the jar. Using a canning funnel, fill the jar with hot syrup to within ¼" of the top and seal with the canning lids and rings. Let cool completely on rack. Remove rings before storing. Label jars and store in a cool place. Refrigerate after opening.

Soda siphons are handy for making all kinds of mixed drinks.

The Soda Siphon

We love our soda siphons! David already had a nice red iSi soda siphon, and at some point, we decided we needed a second one. Nothing is worse than getting everything together for a nice cocktail and finding out the soda siphon is nearly empty. I found a beautiful specimen on eBay, heavy glass surrounded with steel mesh. (I particularly like this one because I can easily see how much water is in it.)

Soda siphons aren't inexpensive. The last time I looked, a new iSi model costs around $50. Then you need CO_2 cartridges to charge or carbonate the water. The siphon holds a full liter of water, and you'll use one cartridge each time you refill it.

I definitely recommend you invest in a soda siphon. It's great any time you make a cocktail calling for soda water or carbonated water. It's better than bottles of carbonated water, which tend to go flat not long after you open them. Do shop around for the cartridges, and buy in bulk if you can. If you buy a box of 10 cartridges, each cartridge costs about a dollar. I like to buy at least ten boxes at a time when I can find them; it's much more economical, they don't take up much cupboard space, and they won't go bad on the shelf.

Ginger Syrup a Jar at a Time

To make ginger syrup one quart at a time, use the following quantities:

- 1½ cups (375 ml) sugar
- 3 cups (750 ml) water
- 1 ounce (30 g) fresh ginger
- Juice and peel of ½ organic lemon

For a stronger ginger taste, leave one slice of ginger in the jar before sealing the lid.

Besides the aforementioned Canadian whiskey and ginger ale (see recipe on page 169), here are a few suggestions for using ginger syrup:

Just Plain Ginger Ale

- 2 shots ginger syrup
- 5 to 6 ounces (150 to 180 ml) soda water

You might also try drizzling ginger syrup over your fruit salad and yogurt in the morning. How about using the ginger syrup in a marinade for pork roast? Once you've tried it, I bet you'll come up with more ways to use this versatile syrup.

Orgeat

This unusual almond concoction is a key ingredient in the Mai Tai (recipe on page 169). It can be hard to find in some areas, so it's worth a try. This is one more ingredient I like making myself because I can have some control over the level of sweetness.

- 2 cups (500 ml) raw almonds, sliced or chopped
- 1½ cups (375 ml) sugar
- 1¼ cups (300 ml) water
- 1 teaspoon (5 ml) orange flower water (or homemade orange bitters)
- 1 ounce (30 ml) vodka

Making Your Own REAL Maraschino Cherries

Admit it, now: the garish, not to say virulent, color of commercial maraschino cherries is a bit frightening, isn't it? Why go to all the trouble of making your own triple-distilled, filtered vodka or bourbon and bitters, only to assemble your handmade cocktail and find that all you have to garnish it with is that neon-pink, overly sugary thing that might or might not actually contain real fruit? You can easily make your own maraschino cherries. And they're good for a lot more than just dropping into a Manhattan. Ice cream comes to mind.

Maraschino Cherries

- Fresh cherries (a sour variety is best), washed and pitted
- Maraschino liqueur or brandy or bourbon

Loosely fill a clean 1-quart Mason jar with cherries. Add maraschino liqueur, brandy or bourbon to completely cover them. Put the lid on the jar and refrigerate. They will be ready to use in about a week. For best flavor, use within a month or so. (Trust me, once a jar of these is opened, you won't have any trouble using them up.)

Note to self: Start making maraschino liqueur in all your spare time.

Crushed almonds left over
from orgeat are perfect for
making tasty macaroons!

Toast almonds at 204°C/400°F for 4 minutes, shaking the pan after 2 minutes.

Cool and grind nuts in food processor or nut grinder.

Heat sugar and water to a boil on medium heat, stirring constantly. Add ground almonds. Reduce heat to low and simmer, stirring often. When mixture is almost boiling, remove from heat and cover. Let it sit at least 3 hours, but not more than 12.

Strain mixture into a bowl. (It will be fairly thick and may drain slowly.) Add flower water and vodka, and bottle.

TIP

The leftover strained almonds make great macaroons! Take 4 egg whites and beat to stiff peaks. Fold whites into the almond mixture. Drop by teaspoonful onto cookie sheets lined with parchment paper. Bake at 176°C/350°F for about 25 minutes, or until macaroons are golden brown. Let cool on sheets before moving to cooling rack. They will be soft but tasty!

Putting It All Together: Classic Cocktail Recipes Featuring Your Homemade Spirits

After you have gone to all the work of making your own spirits, bitters and mixers, what could be better than mixing up (and sharing) a few classic cocktails? There are many good books full of cocktail recipes new, old, and futuristic, and I own a few of them. More often than not, though, I find myself reaching for *The Craft of the Cocktail* (see Books in Appendix A). If you're the type who likes to begin with the basics and work your way up, check it out. In the meantime, try some of these recipes. I've tried to choose ones we particularly like, as well as those that showcase your homemade spirits and mixers.

 ## The Cosmopolitan

We've recently had a lot of fun whipping these up, using handmade citron vodka and orange liqueur. I could go completely gonzo and make my own cranberry juice and grow limes in my greenhouse, but I haven't gotten around to it yet. Be sure to use unsweetened cranberry juice, or the drink can be a bit too sweet.

- 1½ ounces (45 ml) citron vodka (see recipe on page 107)
- ½ ounce (15 ml) homemade orange liqueur (see recipe on page 149)
- 1 organic lime, cut into quarters
- 1 ounce (30 ml) cranberry juice (we like Ocean Spray 100% juice, unsweetened)

Put 3 ice cubes in a cocktail shaker. Squeeze one lime quarter into the shaker and drop it in. Add the vodka and cranberry juice. Put the lid on the shaker and shake until the shaker is feeling frosty. Strain into a cocktail (martini) glass. Bet you can't drink just one. It's got to be healthy with all that fruit.

Ready to start mixing cocktails with homemade spirits, bitters and mixers.

Gin & Tonic

This might seem like a no-brainer. Gin and tonic water, right? You'd be surprised. First, the proportions make a big difference. Order a G & T at a bar, and you're likely to get something heavy on gin and light on tonic. We like a more balanced drink, so there's more tonic evident here. Also, how does anyone think you can make a proper G & T without a lime wedge?

- 1½ ounces (45 ml) gin
- Large lime wedge (¼ lime if the lime is small, ⅛ if it's large)
- Tonic water

Squeeze the lime wedge into a highball glass. Add gin and stir. Add tonic water to within ¾" of the rim, then add ice to fill.

Manhattan

Originally Manhattans were made with rye, which at the time was the predominant whiskey in New York cocktail rooms. Southerners tend to prefer bourbon Manhattans, while others prefer brandy.

- 2 ounces (60 ml) rye whiskey, bourbon or brandy
- 1 ounce (30 ml) sweet vermouth
- 2 dashes Angostura or other aromatic bitters
- Maraschino cherry for garnish (see recipe on page 163)

Put ice in a mixing glass and add the whiskey, vermouth and bitters. Stir as for a martini, then strain into a chilled cocktail glass. Garnish with the cherry.

David's Cuba Libre for Two

- 1 bottle Mexican Coca-Cola (made with sugar, not high fructose corn syrup)
- 2 shots Bacardi Select or other dark rum
- ½ an organic lime, cut into 2 pieces
- 2 dashes Angostura bitters

Put 3 ice cubes in each of two highball or old-fashioned glasses. Squeeze a lime piece into each glass over the ice and drop the lime in. Add the rum, then the bitters and finally the Coca-Cola.

Don't listen to anyone else on this. The bitters make or break a Cuba Libre. If you leave out the bitters, don't tell anyone you learned how to make a Cuba Libre from me!

Dark and Stormy

- 2 ounces (60 ml) dark rum (homemade or Gosling's or Myers's)
- 1½ ounces (45 ml) homemade ginger syrup (see recipe on page 162)

- Soda water from siphon
- Lime wedge

Squeeze the lime into a highball glass and drop it in. Add the rum, ginger syrup and enough soda water to fill within half an inch of the rim. Add ice to fill.

If desired, substitute about 5 ounces of ginger beer for the ginger syrup and soda water.

Old Fashioned

- 1 teaspoon (5 ml) sugar
- 2 dashes Angostura bitters
- 2 orange slices
- 2 maraschino cherries
- Water or soda water
- 2 ounces (60 ml) bourbon

In an old-fashioned glass, muddle the sugar, bitters, one orange slice, one cherry and a splash of water or soda water. Remove the orange and cherry, then add the bourbon, ice and water or soda. Garnish with the remaining orange slice and cherry.

Margarita

- 1½ ounces (45 ml) 100% agave tequila
- 1 ounce (30 ml) Cointreau or homemade brandy-based orange liqueur
- ¼ ounce (7 ml) fresh lime juice

Rub a lime slice on the *outside* of the rim of a chilled cocktail glass. Dip rim in a saucer of coarse salt. Combine ingredients in a mixing glass with ice. Shake well, then strain into the cocktail glass.

Upper Dungeness Whiskey and Ginger Ale

This is one of our favorite drinks, partly because it's just as good hot as cold. In fact, I highly recommend the hot version when you have a cold or the flu. It may not cure you, but it sure makes you care a whole lot less that you're sick. We like Canadian whiskey in this drink, but feel free to experiment with bourbon or other whiskey.

- 1 shot Canadian whiskey
- 1 to 2 shots ginger syrup (2 if you like it sweeter)
- About 3 ounces (90 ml) soda water

Variation: Try Canadian whiskey with *hot* ginger ale. Follow recipe above, substituting boiling water for the soda water, and serve in a mug. We love this on cold winter nights, and it's also great when you have a cold, sinus congestion or flu symptoms.

Mai Tai

- 2 ounces (60 ml) aged homemade dark rum
- ¾ ounce (22 ml) homemade orange liqueur
- ¾ ounce (22 ml) fresh lime juice
- ¼ ounce (7 ml) orgeat (see recipe on page 163)
- Mint sprigs and lime wedge for garnish

Put all ingredients except garnishes into a cocktail shaker with ice. Shake well and strain into an old-fashioned glass filled with ice. Garnish with 2 mint sprigs and a lime wedge.

Champagne Cocktail

- 1 sugar cube
- 4 to 6 dashes Angostura or other aromatic bitters
- Chilled champagne
- Lemon twist for garnish

Put the sugar cube on the bottom of a champagne flute or coupe glass. Soak the sugar cube with the bitters; use more bitters if needed, you want the sugar saturated. Fill the glass with champagne. Garnish with the lemon twist.

Flamed Orange Peel

Thick-skinned navel oranges work best for this. Cut about ½ inch off each end of the orange and stand it on end on a cutting board. Use a sharp paring knife to cut thin oval-shaped twists, about ¾ inch by 1½ inches long, cutting from the middle of the orange toward the bottom. Try to cut so that just a small amount of white pith shows in the middle of the twist; this will maximize the amount of oil that can be squeezed into the drink.

To flame the orange twist, hold a lit match in one hand. Pick up the twist gently with the other hand, holding it by the sides with thumb and forefinger, skin facing down, about four inches above the drink. Hold the match between the twist and the drink, a little closer to the twist. Snap the twist sharply. This will send the oil through the flame and onto the surface of the drink.

Hot Toddy

- ½ ounce (15 ml) brandy, rum or both
- 1 teaspoon (5 ml) honey
- ½ ounce (15 ml) fresh lemon juice

Combine ingredients in a mug and fill with hot water or tea.

Variation: Substitute homemade ginger syrup (see recipe on page 162) for the lemon juice.

Sidecar

- 1 ounce (30 ml) brandy
- 1 ounce (30 ml) orange liqueur
- ¾ ounce (22 ml) fresh lemon juice
- Flamed orange peel for garnish (see method on page 170)

Shake the brandy, liqueur and lemon juice with ice in a cocktail shaker. Strain into a chilled old-fashioned glass. Garnish with the flamed orange peel.

Moscow Mule

- 1½ ounces (45 ml) vodka
- 1½ ounces (45 ml) ginger syrup (see recipe on page 162)
- Carbonated water from a soda siphon
- Lime wedge for garnish

Combine vodka and ginger syrup in a tall iced glass. Add carbonated water to fill, about 3 or 4 ounces (90 to 120 ml). Garnish with lime wedge.

Other Uses for Your Distillation Skills

In case you were wondering, that beautiful still of yours is good for more than just making fantastic liquor. If you're a homesteader or live in a rural area, what about distilling your own water? Distilled water is what you want to put in your flooded-cell batteries (like the 16 deep-cycle batteries in our solar-system battery bank). And of course it's a good idea, no matter where you are, to have an emergency supply of potable water in case of emergencies or disasters. Many people don't know that their water supply may depend on having electrical power; if you're not sure about this, make a point of finding out and being prepared.

We have our own water supply, but what if our pump breaks down and we can't get drinking water to the house? We live far enough away from town and neighbors to opt for distilling water when it's needed.

Distilling Water

Distilling water is quite simple. First make sure your still is super-clean; use the cleaning process in chapter 19 as a guideline. Fill your still's boiling pot ¾ full of water. Heat it to boiling as usual, remembering to turn the condenser's water supply on by the time the water gets to about 66°C/150°F. Make sure the needle valve is wide open; you're not going to be separating anything, just collecting the condensed water vapor. Have a clean jar or bottle in place to collect the distilled water.

Essential Oil Distillation

I mentioned my small Pyrex essential-oil distiller. While I have in fact used this distiller for extracting essential oils and hydrosols, I have also used it on occasion for a small liquor distillation run. It's also handy for distilling small batches of gin, since I can use the plant-material chamber to hold the juniper berries and spices for flavoring the gin.

Essential oils are useful for a lot of things. I used to use them for making my own massage oil blends, as well as homemade soaps, bath salts, that kind of thing. More recently, I have been learning to make a variety of herbal remedies, many using essential oils and infusions of herbs and botanicals. So that little distiller is coming in more and more handy.

I should point out that, while I sometimes use the essential-oil distiller for liquor, I never use the larger still for making essential oils. It doesn't have a chamber for holding plant material for one thing, and it would be a royal pain to clean afterward for another thing. I like things to be efficient, and that little distiller was made specifically for essential-oil production.

We live in an area with a lot of lavender farms and lavender-related businesses. I'm not growing lavender up here yet, but no doubt I will at some point; the climate is ideally suited to it, even at our elevation. Lavender essential oil has many well-known medicinal properties, and I use it a lot for various remedies. I even put a few drops in a spray bottle of water and use it to mist guest-room pillow cases. It's also great for spraying on your broom before sweeping; it helps keep the dust to a minimum and smells great in the process.

Fuel Ethanol

If you were born after 1980, you might think that the recent push to be more "green" is something new. The 1970s, though, was a decade marked by economic hardship and the so-called energy crisis. (Not, of course, that I remember back that far!) In Seattle, where I grew up, Boeing (the major area employer in those pre-Microsoft days) was forced to lay off thousands of workers; remember the billboard that read, "Will the last person leaving Seattle please turn off the lights?" By the mid-1970s, when I was in high school, the back-to-the-land movement was in full swing. New magazines like *Mother Earth News* and *Organic Gardening* provided valuable information to thousands eager to learn how to grow their own food, consume less gasoline and electricity, and generally live simpler, more frugal lives.

Not surprisingly, many people striving for self-sufficiency became interested in making their own backyard fuel, namely ethanol. Don't be deceived by the term "fuel ethanol." Ethanol is ethanol, whether you drink it or put it in your mower's fuel tank. Before long, the government, faced with mounting piles of applications for distilling permits, had to make a decision. Since they were the ones exhorting the masses to use less fuel ("We're in an energy crisis!" they shrilled), they were hardly in a position to make difficulties for enthusiastic do-it-yourselfers willing to do the work of making their own fuel.

So an exception to the usual rules was made, and to this day, the process of obtaining a permit to make fuel ethanol is basically the same. While you do have to file some paperwork, the permit doesn't cost anything. You'll have to explain what you will use to denature your ethanol; you're required to add something to your ethanol that renders it undrinkable, like wood alcohol or high-octane gasoline. Makes sense, I guess, from the suspicious bureaucrat's point of view. The expectation seems to be that if the ethanol isn't denatured, a large percentage of it would be consumed at Happy Hour, not during the daily commute. In any case, the easing of the permit process for fuel ethanol proves that the government is capable of modifying the laws so they make sense; it's just that they rarely seem to have the will to do so.

The first cars ran on ethanol. When gasoline came on the scene, around the time that assembly-line car production was booming and Americans were taking to the roads by the thousands, it soon replaced ethanol as the fuel of choice because it was cheaper. Did you know that racing cars usually run on pure ethanol? With some adjustment to the typical automotive engine, greater speed is possible when ethanol is the fuel because combustion is more complete than with gasoline.

Some cars are in production already that are made to run on ethanol. However, in recent years, gasoline has been so relatively cheap that few in the government seem motivated to pursue alternatives that are (at least at the moment) more expensive. There are books out there, even some government publications (which virtually never go out of print) on the subject of fuel ethanol and how to modify gasoline engines to run on ethanol. Personally I love working on cars, and am intrigued by the challenge of doing some advanced tinkering with carburetors and such; I daresay anyone with good mechanical skills would be able to tackle this project.

Talking of fuel ethanol leads nicely into part of my proposal to change the laws around distilling. Read on for a look at what would happen if we brought back the farm distillery.

The Farm Distillery

Chapters 1 and 2 touched on the economic importance of farm distilleries. I've often wondered: How different would the farm-country landscape be today if Prohibition hadn't happened, along with the oppression of farm distillers that followed? Many thousands of struggling farmers and homesteaders lost their farms when federal agents descended and destroyed their stills. Little did the government care that selling whiskey was, for so many, the only possible means of generating enough cash to pay their property taxes and keep their land for one more lean, belt-tightening year. This expensive, inefficient and ultimately futile endeavor resulted in countless families being forced onto welfare; an appalling and painful example of short-sighted misuse of tax dollars.

Today there are many examples of farm wineries and breweries that are thriving. This could not have happened if laws had not been changed in 1978, allowing private individuals to make "non-commercial" quantities of beer and wine at home. To me it is ridiculous that the government persists in refusing to allow even a small amount of liquor distillation as a hobby. While I am actively working to change the laws to allow limited home distillation, I have a broader dream.

To me, farm distilleries, along with farm wineries and breweries, are the definition of "green" enterprise. Picture a rather small farm or homestead, with maybe just enough space to raise pastured animals and grow corn or other grains to feed the livestock. Some of the grain is used for making whiskey, and the mashed grains are then fed back to the animals. A small methane digester, fed on manure and other farm waste material, is used to generate enough fuel to power the still. The farm store includes a tasting room that attracts tourists, who enthusiastically buy the premium locally produced spirits.

Of course, there would need to be changes to the current laws to allow such things as farm distilleries. Which leads me to...

New York's Farm Distillery Act

Prior to Prohibition, there were hundreds of distilleries in New York state. After Prohibition, there were none. Not one. Ralph Erenzo, who started Tuthilltown Spirits in 2003 (the only farm-based distillery in the state at the time), discovered an obscure law on the books since 2000. This law allowed distillers producing less than 35,000 gallons of liquor annually to be licensed for $1,500 per year. The one-size-fits-all distilling permit previously available cost a whopping $65,000.

Erenzo worked with state legislators to create the Farm Distillery Act of 2007. The bill allows farms to license an on-site distillery. The license requires distillers to source most of their ingredients within New York (Washington has a similar rule for distillers). The farm distillery can have a tasting room and is allowed, unlike large distilleries, to bottle and sell liquor directly to consumers in containers of one quart or less. The spirits may also be sold to wholesalers, restaurants and bars, other farm distilleries or just about anyone licensed to buy. It's important to note that sales have to be face-to-face; no Internet, telephone or mail-order sales allowed. But distillers are allowed to hold tastings, not just at the farm distillery but at events such as state and county fairs, and farmer's markets, and tastings naturally attract tourists as well as local customers.

Since the Farm Distillery Act became law in 2007, at least 40 new farm distilleries have been licensed, and more are planned. In addition, barley and hops production in the state is growing to help meet the demands of distillers and brewers who are required to use locally grown ingredients. Farm distilleries, like farm wineries before them, draw thousands of thirsty tourists every year.

There are additional provisions to the Farm Distillery Act, but you can see the point. The law recognizes what has been known for hundreds of years: Distilled liquor is an agricultural product. Allowing small distilleries on farms ultimately benefits local and state economics, not to mention putting more profits in the farmers' pockets from sales of a true value-added product.

I have heard rumors that a few other states are reviewing similar legislation. I hope so. To me, the historical precedent is clear, and I'm looking forward to a day when farm distilleries are common in Washington State as well.

But I Don't Want a Distillery on My Farm!

At first blush, having a farm distillery and the attendant methane digester might sound just great. However, every time a new piece of equipment is added to the mix, the additional time required to run that equipment and learn new processes has to be taken into account. Small farms and homesteaders may not have the manpower available for yet another chore. This dilemma could be addressed by relegating the distillery to seasonal operation.

But what if the farmer or homesteader simply isn't interested in a distilling operation? After all, it seems to make sense only if the farm is producing enough grain or fruit to justify a distillery. Even then, we've seen the kind of time commitment it can take to end up with a saleable distilled spirit. That's why I'm proposing some kind of central facility, perhaps one to each agricultural county. This facility, which ought to be subsidized by the government, would house one or more commercial stills, maybe an artisan pot still and a column still. Or, if the area's main crops are apples or pears, one still could be an alembic style suitable for making brandy.

This facility could also be used to run classes for hobbyists seeking a non-commercial distilling permit (see my hobby distilling proposal in chapter 25); it could even be a training ground for those wishing to take their hobby to the next level and become licensed commercial distillers. Naturally the facility would create local jobs, since it would require someone with experience to run the distilling operations and teach classes, among other things.

Local farms, especially those not wishing to have their own distilling facilities, could bring their excess or substandard crops to this central facility, to be made into distilled liquor. The mashed grains would then be returned to the farms or resold to others for livestock feed; since this would happen locally, the grain would not need to be dried first, as it is at large commercial distilleries.

Naturally there would be a tasting room at the facility, as well as a retail shop. More jobs created to fill sales positions, tour guides and on and on.

A farm distillery provision in the law is only part of the picture, however. There needs to be provision for people like me, who want to make distilled liquor legally, but not commercially. Chapter 25 outlines my proposal for the addition of a non-commercial distilling permit; part of this proposal is requiring distillers to attend a class. I would be happy to offer my services to assist anyone seeking a distilling permit, provided such a facility existed in which to hold these classes.

Agriculture is a huge industry in Washington State. As of April 2015, there were at least 110 licensed craft distilleries in the state, far more than any other state. One of those distilleries, Dry Fly Distilling in Spokane, has won multiple awards for its whiskey and gin made from locally grown wheat. I heard recently that in the Skagit Valley, north of Seattle, at least 5,000 acres are now planted in barley, specifically for the benefit of local brewers and distillers.

An Example of How a Farm Distillery Law Would Have Made a Difference

This is a real-life example from a few years ago. The numbers aren't exact, based as they are on my memory, but for purposes of this illustration, they are accurate enough.

A friend of mine, who has a nearby small certified-organic farm, was growing wheat among other crops. The first wheat harvest, around 7,000 pounds, had been pre-sold to a local bakery, which planned to use the wheat for making bread. At the last minute, after the grain had been cleaned and stored in sturdy wooden crates, the bakery backed out of the deal. The wheat, it seemed, did not meet their needs in terms of protein content. It would have been satisfactory for pastries, but not for bread.

Well, of course wheat is perishable. Most of that grain, premium certified organic wheat, ended up being sold as feed-grade for less than its actual worth.

If Washington had had a law on the books like New York's Farm Distillery Act, here's how that situation might have played out. That 7,000 pounds of wheat might have been fermented and distilled into, say, three barrels of whiskey. Aged and diluted to 40% ABV, you'd have about 160 gallons of whiskey ready to bottle. That's 64 cases, or 768 bottles. Say you price this premium organic whiskey at $35 (retail, pre-tax) per bottle. You sell it from your farm distillery to local foodies and tourists at full retail price. That comes to gross sales of $26,880. At the current Washington State tax rates, this would amount to tax revenues of $5,727.74.

Say that same grain is sold off for feed. Even if it's sold at $1 per pound (pretty expensive feed), that's gross retail sales of $7,000. Add state sales tax to that, and the tax revenue amounts to $602. Quite a striking difference.

And by the way, if that grain had been used to make whiskey, remember those mashed grains could then have been sold back to local farmers and homesteaders for feeding livestock! It's not a matter of whiskey versus feed, it's more like whiskey *and* feed! Once again, getting two uses out of the same batch of grain just plain makes sense.

Of course, this example doesn't account for labor, investment in equipment and all that, but again, the point should be clear.

One more time: We're talking value-added product here. Local sales tax revenues stay in the local economy; state sales and excise tax revenues go into the state coffers. Local consumers and out-of-town visitors are thrilled to be able to buy a premium local product, boosting community pride. Jobs are created, in an industry making a product that nearly everyone wants to buy. Sounds like a win-win-win proposition to me.

Agriculture and spirits make sense together, on the farm or homestead. It's as true today as it was 200 years ago. If home distilling must be a matter of legislation, it's time to change the laws.

The Case for Making Non-commercial Distilling Legal

In studying the current liquor laws, it is apparent that many of the provisions date back to the Prohibition years (1919–1933) or even earlier. Some of them make no sense today, given that it is legal to make beer and wine at home without restriction. For example, Washington law prohibits the possession of "any mash capable of being distilled into spiritous liquor." Clearly, anyone who makes beer or wine at home is in violation of this part of the law. I suspect that some of the laws are in place now because: a) they are obscure provisions that are rarely, if ever, referred to; and b) it has simply not occurred to anyone to change them.

Let me be clear: I do not believe that completely unrestricted production of alcohol is the answer. I know, from talking to many people as I have traveled in several states speaking on this subject, that there is a widespread belief that it is fine to distill liquor at home as long as it is for private consumption. In addition, I find that once people are made aware of the facts about the current law, the majority of them are eager to comply with the law and want to know how to do so. Unfortunately, the licensing process is unfairly oner-ous for these people, since it is designed for commercial distillers.

As I said, hardly anyone cares about learning from history these days, but if you've read this far, you'll have to agree that the commercial distilling industry began in the home, as a craft. We're way too inclined in this country to discount the importance of anything we can't easily define as a business.

"Home" or "hobby" distillation has been a very popular subject of late. A number of self-published books have appeared in the past several years, more or less subtly encouraging hobbyists to ignore the law and not only to make liquor illegally, but to do so in their homes, a potentially very dangerous thing to do. However, when I applied for a license, I was told that I could not obtain a state distilling license unless I was going to sell the liquor. In other words, I could not get a license to distill liquor as a hobbyist.

It is simply wrong to require all distilling operations to be licensed this way. I believe that if it were easier to obtain the necessary permits, then more people will be inclined to do so. Apparently I am the first person in Washington State to apply for a distillery license while not wishing to pursue distilling commercially, but I am quite positive that I will not be the only one, if a non-commercial permit is made available. This is a perfect time to revisit these laws, revise them where possible and create new ones where necessary.

Chapter 23 gave a brief overview of fuel ethanol production. It wasn't all that many years ago when most Americans either lived on a farm or within a couple of miles of one. And many (if not most) of those farms had some kind of distilling operation. And when cars began to be more widely available, a source of fuel wasn't necessarily handy or cheap. So it made sense that people would be making their own fuel for their cars.

However, then, as in the late 1970s, once gasoline became available in quantity and therefore more cheaply than ethanol, many people quit making fuel ethanol, simply because of the time involved in the process. So much easier to just buy gasoline.

Similarly, for many would-be distillers of potable spirits, it is often cheaper (and, of course, easier) to go out and buy their liquor ready-to-drink. Ours is a capitalistic culture, and capitalism always values quantity over quality. Thus the fuel-ethanol naysayers cannot grasp the concept that small-scale ethanol production might, in fact, be even more efficient than large-scale production.

A bushel of corn can yield 2½ gallons of ethanol, along with (I know, I harp on this too) about 18 pounds of high-protein feed. If you live in corn country, numbers like these are encouraging. And the fact that the government has seen fit to allow ethanol distillation for fuel without requiring permit or bond fees is a good sign too. What doesn't make sense to me is why, if we can make ethanol destined for a fuel tank, we're still not allowed to make exactly the same ethanol if we admit it's destined to be served up in a martini glass?

Dear Uncle Sam: Why Can I Make Beer and Wine but Not Distilled Spirits?

As I expected, regarding home distillation of liquor, the government's stated concerns (read: justification) fall into two categories: Safety issues and tax revenue issues.

Oh, goody. Here we go.

Safety Issues

Having made a lot of beer and wine over the years myself, I do get that there are safety issues with distilling that do not apply to wine or beer. Think about it: If you screw up something when you make beer or wine, what's the worst that can happen? You have bad-tasting beer or wine. I guess if you really screw up and bottle something before it's fermented, you can be faced with a room full of exploding bottles.

Distilling is different. Did you know that the first distillate to come out of your still will be around 95% alcohol? That's nearly as volatile as gasoline. If you're not careful, or you're in a hurry and overheat your still, the alcoholic vapor escaping from the condenser presents a real danger of explosion. When you're doing spirit runs, handling low wines of 30% alcohol or more, you must be very careful not to let any of those low wines (or the distillate coming from the still) get anywhere near your heat source, for fear of fire or explosion.

In addition, safe distillation depends on the distiller's skill in making the cuts, that is, separating the poisonous and bad-tasting stuff from the potable ethanol. There is a lot of science that, when mastered, helps in this process, but there remains a subjective element to distilling as well, which comes down to choices made at critical junctures by the thoughtful distiller.

Tax Revenue Issues

I'd love to debate this point with anyone at all. I promise, the numbers are on my side here. As stated below, the critical point of my proposal is to limit the size of still that a hobby distiller may use; everything else falls into place once this limit is defined. Believe me, limiting the size of the still automatically limits the amount of distilled liquor you can make. You can't just turn the heat up and have everything run faster; there are safety concerns with doing that (see chapter 10), and in my experience, that's counter-productive; alcohol yields actually drop, due to some of the alcohol escaping from the condenser as vapor.

As an example, the boiling pot on my still holds a maximum of 28 liters or about 7 gallons. The most I ever put in the still, though, is about 15 liters, which is less than two-thirds of the pot capacity. This is a safety measure to minimize the risk of boilovers. I'm not kidding, I could run this still 24/7, at a safe rate, and I wouldn't come close to making even 100 gallons of liquor in a year. And obviously no one is going to be running their stills that much. We're talking hobbyists here, who will most likely be using their stills in their spare time, say half a day every weekend, or less.

Apparently the government assumes that if we are allowed to make even a tiny amount of our own booze, we'll stop buying liquor altogether. That's just not the case. (See chapter 7 for more on this topic.) Frankly, if hobby distillers are able to make enough liquor, in their spare time, to meet all their needs for potent potables, then it stands to reason they weren't buying that much from the liquor stores in the first place. You tell me: How much tax revenue did the state lose when those few consumers stopped spending money at the liquor store?

Let me put things in more concrete terms. Say I buy 6 bottles of spirits every month, at an average (pre-tax) price of $22. That's $132 per month. I live in Washington State, so add $44.04 in taxes to that number, every month. That's a total of $528.48 just in *taxes* every year! (Remember that the state is also collecting fees at the distributor and retailer level on the same liquor.)

I swear, even with all the distilling I have been doing in the course of the very enjoyable research for this book, I'm not making anywhere near 6 bottles of ready-to-drink spirits every month. (I refer you again to the discussion in chapter 7.) And I don't have a full-time job! I can't imagine most hobbyists having the time to make more than a few bottles a month, and that's after they have some experience and their yields improve. No, the argument that hobby distilling will take significant amounts of tax dollars out of the hands of the government just doesn't make any sense.

My Proposal, Part 1:
Create a Non-commercial State Distilling Permit

From my experience in attempting to license a tiny distilling facility on our farm, it is obvious that the current licensing system is unfair to people like me, who want to distill small amounts of liquor legally, but not commercially. My proposal addresses the stated needs of the government, while allowing non-commercial distillers like myself to pursue our interest in production of high-quality craft spirits while complying with the law.

Major points of this permit would be:

• A limit on the size of still allowed, perhaps a boiling-pot capacity of 30 liters

- Limit annual production of distilled spirits to, say, 75 proof gallons
- Require attendance at a class to show understanding of safety issues, facility requirements, etc.
- Require registration of the still and a floor plan of the distilling facility
- Require a 1-page application and a reasonable annual fee, say $45
- Sales of liquor not allowed
- Safety rules for distilleries must be followed (fire extinguishers, etc.)
- Distillers should be encouraged to use ingredients sourced in Washington, as required for other Washington State distillery licenses

My Proposal, Part 2:
No Federal Permit Needed For Non-commercial Distillers

My idea for dealing with distilling permits at the federal level is quite simple. It amounts to an exemption: Anyone making no more than, say, 100 gallons of distilled liquor annually (or the maximum allowed under the distiller's state law, whichever is smaller) would not need a Federal Basic Permit.

This exemption would have only one caveat: the assumption that the individual is in compliance with his or her state's laws. For example, if I obtain a non-commercial distilling permit in Washington State, presumably I would need to show a copy of this permit to the federal inspector. I would not have that permit unless I complied with the limit on the size of still, and the other provisions outlined above, so there would be no need to go through all that again.

Now really, was that so difficult? Someone told me recently that it's often easier to introduce a new law than it is to amend an existing one. Maybe that's true, or more true now than it used to be. Somehow this was managed back in 1978, when the law was changed to allow home beer- and wine-making. The Washington State Liquor

Control Board managed to introduce a new lower-cost Craft Distillery license in 2008, and look what that's done for the Washington economy!

This year and in 2016, I will be traveling in several states to speak on this subject at events such as the Mother Earth News Fair (motherearthnewsfair.com). I am going to continue my efforts to change the laws. Once Washington State finds the will to make the necessary changes to the laws, I confidently expect other states to follow suit. Ditto for Canada. I'm ready to present my case to anyone, at any time. I'm not afraid of the government, or intimidated by the majesty of the law, because I know the facts are on my side.

This is a perfect time to revisit these laws, revise them where possible and create new ones where necessary. I didn't set out to be a trailblazer, but here I am. Someone has to take the initiative when the laws are so demonstrably unfair, outdated and just plain silly. If I can be that person in this case, then damn the paperwork, full speed ahead!

Let's Raise the Bar:
The Future of
True Craft Distilling

In early December 2014, I met with Kevin Van de Wege, a Washington State legislator in our area, to talk about the distillery licensing process. He graciously listened to my concerns, and sympathized with a summary of my experience trying to obtain a distilling permit. I showed him my proposal for changing the laws, and he agreed to look into it for me when the legislature was back in session.

My proposal has changed somewhat since then. I've learned a lot in the course of researching this book, with the result that I am more convinced than ever of the strength of my position.

Just a few days before I turned in this manuscript, I got a call from Mr. Van de Wege. He said he had spoken to one or two people at the Washington State Liquor Control Board. The response he got was basically that they couldn't see any way of changing the state laws while still being in compliance with federal laws.

This makes no sense to me at all. Since before Prohibition, the federal government has left it to the individual states to enact and enforce their own liquor control laws. I don't necessarily think this is a bad system; I just think the federal government should have no jurisdiction over non-commercial distilling.

To sum up: In the United States, we have been allowed to make beer and wine at home since 1978. In New Zealand, old legislation was scrapped in 1996, making it legal for hobbyists to make distilled liquor at home without a permit. The Farm Distillery Act was signed into law in 2007 in New York state, allowing small distillery operations on farms to be licensed for a lot less money, resulting in amazing economic benefits in just the first few years. Allowing limited home liquor distillation is the next logical step. The government needs to admit that the current laws are unfair to people like you and me, and someone needs to find the will to deal with it.

The flaw in the system has been brought out into the clear light of day. I have proposed a solution that addresses the stated government concerns, while allowing people like you and me to pursue a fascinating hobby legally. It is clear that such changes will ultimately benefit distillers, farmers, consumers, retailers who provide the necessary equipment, supplies and ingredients, local tourism and the local and state government as well.

It's time to go back to the future and put the "craft" back in craft distilling. I'm not giving up. Oh, no. I'm just getting started.

Useful Resources

Books

Good Spirits: A New Look at Ol' Demon Alcohol
by Gene Logsdon, Chelsea Green, 1999
I love Gene Logsdon. I found a used copy of this book and have read it through at least half a dozen times. Gene relates some instructive (and often poignant) stories, some from his own family, about the consequences of oppressive liquor taxes and regulations in America. He makes a strong case for the re-legalization of home distilling, so naturally he is my hero.

Making Pure Corn Whiskey (2nd Edition)
by Ian Smiley, Amphora Society, 2003
Includes detailed instructions for building a fractionating still, recipes and techniques for several kinds of whiskey, and interesting techniques like distilling pure ethanol. Excellent reference for hobby distillers from a distiller in New Zealand, where unlicensed home distilling is legal.

The Art of Distilling Whiskey and other Spirits: An Enthusiast's Guide to the Artisan Distilling of Potent Potables
Bill Owens and Alan Dikty, Editors, Quarry Books, 2009
This is not a how-to on distilling. It details the processes of how whiskey, gin, vodka, brandy, tequila, rum and liqueurs are made commercially. Includes a section profiling some craft and artisan distillers in the US. Beautiful photography and an entertaining writing style.

Craft of Whiskey Distilling
by Bill Owens, American Distilling Institute, 2009
This is the only distilling book I've seen that has any information about the licensing process. Definitely geared toward those interested in starting a commercial distillery, it explains in detail the process of turning

grain into top-quality whiskey. Includes a to-do list, a 3-year business plan, a sample distillery floor plan, even a quiz on distilling and the distilling industry.

Distilling Fruit Brandy
by Josef Pischl, Schiffer Publishing, 2012
Excellent guide for making top-quality fruit brandies. Explains everything from choosing fruit to fermenting and distilling. There are definite differences in the mashing and distilling processes compared to other spirits, so I highly recommend this book if you're interested in making brandy.

Bitters: A Spirited History of a Classic Cure-all
by Brad Thomas Parsons, Ten Speed Press, 2011
Much more than just the history of bitters, this book includes recipes for classic bitters such as orange and grapefruit, and interesting ones such as coffee-pecan and husk cherry bitters. Lots of cocktail recipes that use your homemade bitters too. About time a whole book was devoted to this subject.

The Drunken Botanist: The Plants That Create the World's Great Drinks
by Amy Stewart, Algonquin Books of Chapel Hill, 2013
This book is surprisingly hard to put down once you start reading. A whole lot of fascinating facts about the trees, shrubs, herbs, spices and other plant-based ingredients that contribute character and flavor to any alcoholic spirit you can think of. Highly recommended for anyone who's truly into top-quality spirits and cocktails.

The Craft of the Cocktail
by Dale DeGroff, Clarkson Potter Publishers, 2002
Excellent resource for everything you need to know to stock your bar and mix cocktails like an expert, by the expert himself: Dale DeGroff, legendary mixologist of the Rainbow Room in New York City. You should buy this book just for the awesome Bloody Mary Buffet; I have plans to throw this kind of party this summer. Guess I better start making more vodka.

Books You Might Want to Avoid

Out of curiosity mostly, and partly for market research, I have bought some of these. Quite a few have appeared on the market recently: mostly self-published, smallish books that encourage stove-top distillation and discourage legal distilling. The ones I have, every single one of them, seem not to have had much proofreading, much less editing. They usually include a disclaimer saying that distillation without a license is illegal and the book is meant for entertainment purposes only. Yeah, right. Some have deceptive titles; others fail to deliver on the promise of their online descriptions. At least look at the reviews before you fork over the cash. You've been warned.

Ingredients

Yeast, Enzymes, etc.
Hillbilly Stills: Turbo yeast and yeast ingredients, plus other specialized yeasts, some available in large quantities. (hillbillystills.com)

Prestige brand yeast: whiskeyyeast.com

Still Spirits: Pre-packaged mixes of distilling yeast, yeast nutrients and amylase enzymes. stillspirits.com

The Grape and Granary: distilling yeasts, amylase and rhysozyme enzymes, filtering supplies like the Carbon Snake, and other distilling-related stuff. thegrape.net

Herbs, Spices and Other Botanicals
Depending on where you live, you can often pick up quite a good selection of herbs, spices, etc. at your local natural foods store. Of course, you can order online, and some ingredients are harder to find locally, but do try to buy locally whenever you can.

Starwest Botanicals (starwestbotanicals.com) has a huge selection of herbs, spices, dried citrus peel, tree barks and other botanical ingredients. They also sell essential oils. Many organic varieties available too, and not just in tiny quantities. Excellent source, and one of my favorites.

Tenzing Momo (tenzingmomo.com)
Good source for cinchona bark, as well as many other botanical ingredients and essential oils.

Websites

The usual caveat about websites applies here: Things on the Internet can and do change frequently, so I apologize in advance if you try one of these links round about 2032 and can't access the page. I promise that I checked all of these links right before the book went to press.

Distilled spirits permits: ttb.gov/spirits/index.shtml
Laws and regulations: ttb.gov/spirits/spirits_regs.shtml
Washington State Liquor Control Board: liq.wa.gov
State alcohol boards: ttb.gov/wine/control_board.shtml

See Appendix B for more information on licensing in Canada.

Resources for Information on Distilling in Canada

In Canada, liquor licenses are issued by the legal authority of each province to allow an individual or business to manufacture alcoholic beverages. Many regulations apply to all types of liquor licenses that are available within each province. License holders must strictly follow all the terms and rules to avoid fines for non-compliance or revocation of the license.

Distillers in Canada

The website canadianwhisky.org maintains a list of craft distillers in Canada.

Tip: The Agriculture and Agri-food Canada website (agr.gc.ca) has good information about distilling in Canada. Click on the Processed Food and Beverages link on the left to find distillery information.

Licensing Information by Province

Alberta

The Alberta Gaming and Liquor Commission (AGLC) licenses liquor activities in Alberta. In 1993, the AGLC, which regulates Alberta's liquor industry, was privatized, enabling the private sector to retail, warehouse and distribute liquor in the province.

Five classes of licenses, as well as a special event license, are issued for the sale and manufacture of liquor. The relevant license for hobby distillers is:

- **Class E license** (for liquor manufacturing)

See also: AGLC handbook, aglc.ca/pdf/handbooks/liquor_licensee_hand book.pdf

British Columbia

The British Columbia government regulates and monitors the liquor industry to protect the public from the harm that may be caused by making and selling liquor or products that contain liquor. The Liquor Control and Licensing Branch (LCLB) regulates liquor service in bars and restaurants, private liquor stores, liquor manufacturers and importers, Ubrews and UVins (for personal liquor manufacturing), as well as liquor service at special occasion events. Inspectors will visit establishments unannounced, and if the establishment fails to comply with laws and regulations, seizure of liquor, fine or suspension of license may follow.

Manitoba

Established in 1923, the Manitoba Liquor Control Commission serves as a regulating agency of alcohol sales and distributions. Its licensing board provides 12 types of liquor license applications, including Dining Room License, Cocktail Lounge License and Spectator Activities License. Beside basic requirements for licensed premises such as proper seating capacities, the licensing board also reviews criminal record checks and security plans before issuing a liquor license.

Nova Scotia

Established in 1930, and headquartered in Halifax, the Nova Scotia Liquor Corporation (NSLC) is the sole distributor and runs all retail outlets selling alcohol, except for four private wine specialty shops, and, in rural areas where there is not an NSLC location, 23 private "agency" liquor stores. The former Liquor Commission was restructured as a Crown corporation and became the Liquor Corporation.

Information about obtaining a distilling license can be found on the NSLC website, mynslc.com/Content_CommunicationsPages/Content _Footer/Content_Services/Permits.aspx

Ontario

The Liquor Licensing Board of Ontario (LLBO) was the regulatory agency responsible for issuing liquor permits and regulating the sale, service and consumption of alcoholic beverages to promote moderation and responsible use within the province. Established in 1947 under the Liquor License Act (Ontario), the agency is not to be confused with the Liquor

Control Board of Ontario (LCBO), an alcohol retailer. The LLBO was re-placed by the Alcohol and Gaming Commission of Ontario in 1998 under the Alcohol and Gaming Regulation and Public Protection Act (Ontario), passed in 1996.The LLBO name lives on in many eateries and entertain-ment establishments which display official certification to indicate the location is legally licensed to serve alcohol.

Quebec

The province of Quebec has its own special laws concerning selling liquor and acquiring a liquor license. The Régie des alcools, des courses et des jeux is in charge of liquor distribution and sets the laws on liquor con-sumption. The permits authorizing the sale or service of alcoholic bever-ages within the territory concerning liquor permits concluded between the Government and a Mohawk community are determined in the agree-ment and issued by the authority designated in the agreement.

Saskatchewan

The Saskatchewan Liquor and Gaming Authority is the corporation re-sponsible for the distribution and regulation of alcohol. Businesses seeking authorization to serve alcoholic beverages must complete the Commercial Liquor Permit Application.

Commercial liquor licenses issued in Saskatchewan:

- Tavern License: Issued primarily for the purpose of selling alcohol in public establishments including bars, pubs, restaurants and night-clubs.
- Special Use License: Issued for restaurants that do not primarily focus on alcoholic beverages but are served on special occasions.
- Manufacturer License: Issued to authorize applicants with establish-ments primarily based on the manufacturing of alcoholic beverages.

Sample Record-keeping Form

See the following page for a sample liquor production record sheet you can photocopy and use to help you keep track of your distilling process.

Simplified Distilled Liquor Production Record

Type of Spirit: _____ Recipe used: _____

Mashing

Backset or acid added (type and amount) _____ Adjusted water pH _____

Enzymes added (type and amount) _____

Fermentation

Start date _____ Wash amt _____ OG _____ End date _____ TG _____

Yeast type _____ Yeast amount _____

Distilling — Stripping run

Date _____ Wash amount _____ Est. ABV _____ Start time _____

First distillate (time) _____ Low wines collected (ml) _____ Low wines ABV _____

Distilling — Spirit run #1

Date _____ Amt low wines _____ ABV _____ Start time _____

First distillate (time) _____ Heads collected _____ Hearts cut time _____

Hearts collected _____ Tails cut time _____ Tails collected _____

Distilling — Spirit run #2 (Irish whiskey)

Date _____ Amt hearts _____ ABV _____ Start time _____

First distillate (time) _____ Heads collected _____ Hearts cut time _____

Hearts collected _____ Tails cut time _____ Tails collected _____

Distilling — Spirit run #3 (Vodka, Gin)

Date _____ Amt hearts _____ ABV _____ Start time _____

First distillate (time) _____ Heads collected _____ Hearts cut time _____

Hearts collected _____ Tails cut time _____ Tails collected _____

Aging

American oak ____ French oak ____ Other _____

Toasted _____ Charred _____

Start date _____ End date _____

Comments

_____

_____

_____

Index

About the Author

VICTORIA REDHED MILLER is a writer, photographer and home-steader who lives on a 40-acre off-grid farm in the foothills of Washington's Olympic Mountains with her husband David. She strives to enhance her family's self-reliance through solar energy, gardening, raising heritage poultry, craft brewing and distilling, blacksmithing, and other traditional skills. Victoria blogs about her experiences at canyoncreekfarms.blogspot.com. She is the author of *Pure Poultry: Living Well with Heritage Chickens, Turkeys and Ducks*.

If you have enjoyed *Craft Distilling*, you might also enjoy other

Books to Build a New Society

Our books provide positive solutions for people who
want to make a difference. We specialize in:

Climate Change ◆ Conscious Community
Conservation & Ecology ◆ Cultural Critique
Education & Parenting ◆ Energy ◆ Food & Gardening
Health & Wellness ◆ Modern Homesteading & Farming
New Economies ◆ Progressive Leadership ◆ Resilience
Social Responsibility ◆ Sustainable Building & Design

New Society Publishers
ENVIRONMENTAL BENEFITS STATEMENT

New Society Publishers has chosen to produce this book on recycled paper made
with 100% post consumer waste, processed chlorine free, and old growth free.

For every 5,000 books printed, New Society saves the following resources:[1]

28	Trees
2,562	Pounds of Solid Waste
2,818	Gallons of Water
3,676	Kilowatt Hours of Electricity
4,656	Pounds of Greenhouse Gases
20	Pounds of HAPs, VOCs, and AOX Combined
7	Cubic Yards of Landfill Space

[1]Environmental benefits are calculated based on research done by the Environmental Defense Fund and
other members of the Paper Task Force who study the environmental impacts of the paper industry.

For a full list of NSP's titles, please call 1-800-567-6772 or check out our web site at:

www.newsociety.com

new society
PUBLISHERS